Sew Gifts!

25 HANDMADE GIFT IDEAS FROM TOP DESIGNERS

Martingale
Create with Confidence

Sew Gifts!:
25 Handmade Gift Ideas from Top Designers
© 2013 by Martingale®

Martingale
19021 120th Ave. NE, Ste. 102
Bothell, WA 98011-9511 USA
ShopMartingale.com

CREDITS

President and CEO: Tom Wierzbicki
Editor in Chief: Mary V. Green
Design Director: Paula Schlosser
Managing Editor: Karen Costello Soltys
Acquisitions Editor: Karen M. Burns
Technical Editor: Laurie Baker
Copy Editor: Tiffany Mottet
Production Manager: Regina Girard
Cover and Interior Designer: Adrienne Smitke
Photographer: Brent Kane
Illustrator: Christine Erikson

Printed in China
18 17 16 15 14 13   8 7 6 5 4 3 2 1

Library of Congress Cataloging-in-Publication Data
is available upon request.

ISBN: 978-1-60468-301-1

Contents

Introduction

Something wonderful happens when you sew gifts for people. You begin by thinking about what they might like, how they might use it, what colors or styles would be most appreciated. You ponder fabric and color options and plan the construction. The sewing itself might be simple or complex; it doesn't matter, because you love to sew and you enjoy it even more when you do it with someone special in mind. And then there's joy that comes when you deliver your heartfelt gift and see the recipient's pleasure at receiving it.

This book features almost as many types of gifts as there are occasions to give them. Whether it's a pretty and practical zippered bag for Mother's Day, a clever fabric game board for Christmas, or a knitting needle case "just because," you'll find just the right gift here. The projects were created for you by an impressive group of talented designers, and they range from a whimsical pincushion to a playful bake set to an elegant scarf stitched from kimono silk. Whether you're an expert sewist or are just developing your skills, you'll find the information and inspiration you need to make wonderful, creative gifts for everyone on your list!

- *Mary V. Green*

> This trendy tote is eye-catching for sure, but it's also roomy enough to carry a sewing project or a stack of library books. The chevron patchwork pockets are fun to make and will help you keep all of your belongings organized and close at hand.
>
> ~Sarah

Chevron TOTE BAG

FINISHED BAG: 12" x 14½"

Designed and made by Sarah Minshall

MATERIALS

Yardage is based on 42"-wide fabric unless otherwise noted.

1⅛ yards of white solid for main tote piece, chevron pockets, pocket backing, and pocket binding

⅝ yard of coordinating print for straps and lining

⅛ yard *each* of yellow, green, blue, and turquoise solids for chevron pockets

14" x 28" piece of batting

½ yard of 45"-wide fusible fleece

⅝ yard of 20"-wide fusible heavyweight interfacing

CUTTING

From the white solid, cut:
12 squares, 3" x 3"
2 strips, 1" x 12½"
2 strips, 2" x 12½"
2 squares, 14" x 14"
2 rectangles, 12½" x 15"
2 strips, 2½" x 13"

From *each* of the yellow, green, blue, and turquoise solids, cut:
12 squares, 3" x 3" (48 total)

From the batting, cut:
2 squares, 14" x 14"

From the coordinating print, cut:
2 strips, 3" x 42"
2 rectangles, 12½" x 15"

From the fusible fleece interfacing, cut:
2 rectangles, 12½" x 15"

From the fusible heavyweight interfacing, cut:
4 strips, 3" x 21"

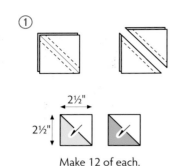

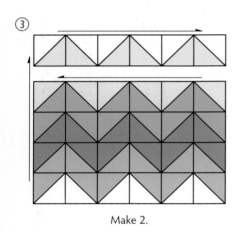

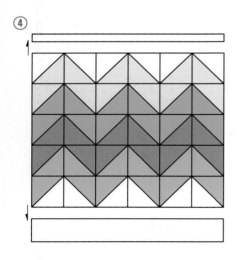

①

2½"

2½"

Make 12 of each.

②

Make 12 of each.

③

Make 2.

④

MAKING THE CHEVRON POCKETS

Use a ¼"-wide seam allowance throughout.

1 Use a pencil and ruler to draw a diagonal line from corner to corner on the wrong side of each white, yellow, green, blue, and turquoise 3" square.

2 Pair each of six yellow and six turquoise 3" squares with a marked white square, right sides together. Stitch ¼" from both sides of the marked lines. Cut the pairs apart on the marked lines. Each pair will yield two half-square-triangle units. Press the seam allowances toward the yellow and turquoise triangles. Square up each unit to 2½" x 2½". ①

3 Pair each of the remaining yellow squares with a green square, and each of the remaining turquoise squares with a blue square, right sides together. Stitch, cut, press, and trim as described in step 2. In the same manner, pair each of the remaining green squares with a blue square; stitch, cut, press, and trim as before. ②

4 Arrange six half-square-triangle units of each combination into horizontal rows as shown. Sew the units in each row together. Press the seam allowances in opposite directions from row to row. Sew the rows together. Press the seam allowances in one direction. Repeat to make a total of two pieced pocket units. ③

5 Sew a white 1" x 12½" strip to the top of each pocket unit from step 4 and a white 2" x 12½" strip to the bottom of each unit. Press the seam allowances toward the strips. ④

6 Place a white 14" backing square on your work surface, wrong side up. Layer a 14" batting square over the backing square, followed by a pocket unit from step 5, right side up. Baste the layers together. Quilt ¼" from the diagonal lines of each half-square-triangle unit, or as desired. Trim the batting and backing even with the pieced top. Repeat with the remaining pieced unit to make a total of two pocket pieces. Square up the pockets to 12½" x 12½", if needed.

7 Press each of the white 2½" x 13" strips in half lengthwise, wrong sides together. Stitch a folded strip to the top of each pocket unit, aligning the raw edges and having a small amount of excess strip extending at each end. Wrap each strip over the top edge of the pocket piece to the wrong side. Hand stitch the folded edge to the pocket backing. Trim the ends even with the sides of the pocket.

MAKING THE MAIN TOTE PIECE

1 Follow the manufacturer's instructions to fuse a 12½" x 15" fleece rectangle to the wrong side of each white 12½" x 15" rectangle.

2 Follow the manufacturer's instructions to fuse two heavyweight interfacing 3" x 21" strips end to end to the wrong side of each coordinating

print 3" x 42" strap strip. Make sure to butt the interfacing ends so there are no gaps, but don't overlap them.

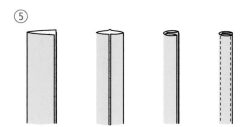

3 Press each strap strip in half lengthwise, wrong sides together. Open up each strip and fold the long edges toward the center crease; press again. Fold the strip in half along the original center crease. The straps should now measure ¾" wide. Edgestitch ⅛" from both long edges. ⑤

4 Pin a strap to the right side of each interfaced rectangle from step 1, beginning and ending at the bottom of the rectangle and positioning the edges 3" from each side. Make sure the straps aren't twisted. Stitch the straps in place along the previous edge-stitching line, starting at the bottom edge and sewing 13½" up the strap, and then across the strap and back down the other side. Repeat on the opposite end of the strap. ⑥

ASSEMBLING THE TOTE

1 Place a main tote piece right side up on your work surface. Pin a chevron pocket, right side up, over the main tote piece, aligning the lower edges and sides. Baste the pocket in place along the outer edges. Repeat for the remaining main tote piece and pocket.

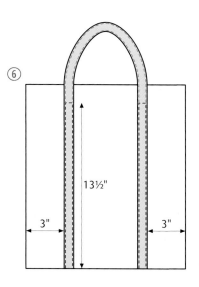

2 With right sides together, sew a coordinating print 12½" x 15" lining rectangle to each piece from step 1 along the top edge only, keeping the straps out of the stitching. Press the seam allowances toward the coordinating print rectangles.

3 Open up the pieces from step 2 so that the outer panels and lining are separated, except at the top where they are stitched together. Pin the pieces right sides together, lining to lining and main tote piece to main tote piece. Sew around the perimeter, leaving a 4" opening along the bottom of the lining for turning. ⑦

4 Turn the tote right side out through the opening in the lining. Slip-stitch the lining closed and topstitch ¼" from the top edge of the tote.

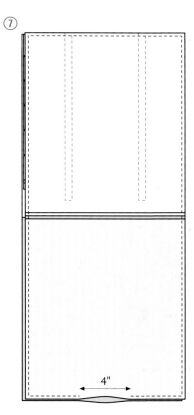

Zippered Dresden
POUCH

 *Adding a little extra touch, like half of a Dresden Plate, can take a simple zippered pouch from really nice to super special. Plus, it's a great way to use up scraps. I like to use a textured fabric, like linen or Quilter's Linen by Robert Kaufman, for the exterior of my pouches to add visual interest.*

~Elizabeth

FINISHED POUCH: 10" x 6"

Designed and made by Elizabeth Dackson

MATERIALS

Fat quarters measure 18" x 21".

1 fat quarter of pink linen or tone-on-tone print for pouch exterior
1 fat quarter of contrasting or coordinating print for pouch lining
Scraps of 10 assorted fabrics, no smaller than 2" x 3", for Dresden Plate wedges
5" x 5" square of pink print for Dresden Plate center
5" x 5" square of neutral-color fabric for Dresden Plate center backing
3" x 3" square of contrasting fabric for zipper tabs
18" x 22" rectangle of fusible medium-weight interfacing
10"- to 12"-long red zipper
Fabric marking pen or pencil

CUTTING

From the assorted scraps, cut a *total* of:
10 Dresden wedges (page 13)

From the fusible medium-weight interfacing, cut:
2 rectangles, 7" x 11"

From the pink linen or tone-on-tone print, cut:
2 rectangles, 7" x 11"

From the contrasting or coordinating print, cut:
2 rectangles, 7" x 11"

MAKING THE DRESDEN PLATE APPLIQUÉ

Use a ¼"-wide seam allowance throughout, unless otherwise noted.

1 Fold each Dresden wedge in half lengthwise, right sides together, aligning the raw edges. Use your fingernail to slightly crease the fold. Sew across the widest end of the wedge, backstitching at the fold. Trim the folded corner at an angle. Finger-press the seam allowances open. ①

2 Turn each wedge right side out and use a chopstick or point turner to create a nice pointy tip. Line up the seam of each wedge with the crease created in step 1; press using a hot, dry iron. ②

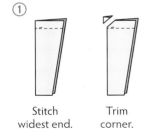

①

Stitch widest end. Trim corner. Finger press.

②

Press.

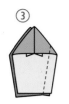

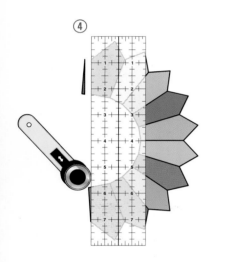

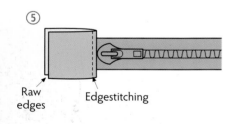

Raw
edges

Edgestitching

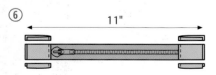

11"

3 Randomly arrange the 10 wedges in a semicircle. Join the wedges in pairs along the long edges, and then sew the pairs together to complete the semicircle. Press the seam allowances open. ③

4 Align a quilting ruler with the outer points of the semicircle's end wedges as shown; trim to create a straight edge. ④

ASSEMBLING THE POUCH

1 Follow the manufacturer's instructions to fuse the interfacing rectangles to the wrong sides of the exterior 7" x 11" rectangles.

2 Fold one of the interfaced exterior rectangles in half crosswise, wrong sides together, to make a piece 5½" x 7"; lightly crease the fold. Open up the piece so the right side is up. Position the Dresden Plate appliqué on the rectangle, right side up, aligning the appliqué raw edges with the top of the rectangle and the appliqué center seam with the crease. Pin the appliqué in place. Use your favorite appliqué method to stitch the Dresden Plate in place around the outer pointed edges. Elizabeth used a narrow zigzag to appliqué her piece.

3 Trace the semicircle pattern on page 13 onto the wrong side of the neutral 5" square. Place the square right sides together with the pink print square. Stitch around the curved edges of the semicircle, leaving the straight edge open. Cut out the semicircle, adding a ¼"-wide seam allowance to the curved edge. Clip the curve and turn the semicircle to the right side; press.

4 Position the semicircle over the Dresden Plate center, aligning the semicircle raw edge with the top of the rectangle and overlapping the raw edges at the narrow ends of the wedges. Appliqué the semicircle in place along the finished edges using your favorite method. Set the appliquéd front piece aside.

5 To prepare the zipper, fold the contrasting fabric 3" square in half; press. Cut the folded piece in half crosswise, from the folded edge to the raw edges, to yield two zipper tabs. Place one tab across the tape ends at the zipper-pull end of the zipper as shown. Edgestitch ⅛" from the fold (you may have to unzip your zipper a tiny bit). ⑤

6 Measuring from the end of the zipper tab, trim the zipper to measure 9¾" long. Sew the remaining zipper tab to the opposite end of the zipper, overlapping the zipper-tape ends ¼". The zipper should now measure 11" from tab end to tab end. Trim the sides of the zipper tabs even with the sides of the zipper tape. ⑥

7 Place a lining rectangle right side up on your cutting mat, then place the zipper on top, face up, aligning the tape edges with the upper edge of the rectangle. Place the appliquéd pouch front over the zipper, right side down. Pin the pieces together. Using a zipper foot, sew along the upper edge to attach the zipper. Repeat with the remaining exterior and lining rectangles, sandwiching the opposite side of the zipper between them. Press the seam allowances away from the zipper. From the outside, topstitch through all layers on both sides of the zipper.

8 Unzip the zipper. Open up the pieces so the pouch front and back are right sides together, the lining pieces are right sides together, and the zipper tapes fold over on themselves with the zipper teeth toward the bag fabric, not the lining. Be sure to pin where the exterior and lining pieces meet the zipper to eliminate shifting as much as possible. Using a ½"-wide seam allowance, stitch around the piece, leaving a 4" opening in the bottom of the lining for turning. ⑦

9 To box the corners, grab one of the lining corners and align the top and bottom seams. Press with a hot, dry iron. Measure 1½" from the tip of the corner and draw a line. Sew across this line, and then trim the excess corner fabric to approximately ¼". Repeat for the remaining lining corner and the two exterior bag corners. ⑧

10 Pull the lining and exterior fabrics through the zipper opening. Use a chopstick to push out all of your seams. Press as needed. Slip-stitch the opening in the lining closed. Tuck the finished lining into the pouch, and voilà! You're all done!

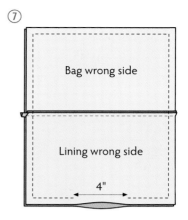

⑦

Bag wrong side

Lining wrong side

4"

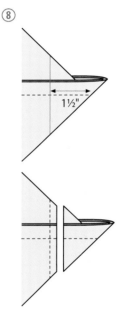

⑧

1½"

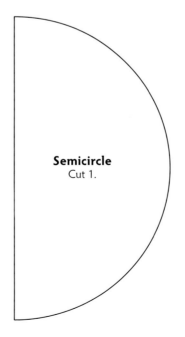

¼" seam allowance

Dresden wedge
Cut 10.

Semicircle
Cut 1.

Semicircle pattern does not include seam allowance.

When you just need to carry a few necessities with you, this little wallet fits the bill. Just the right size for a driver's license or student ID card, some pocket money, and a house key, it fits neatly in a pocket so you don't have to carry a purse. A snap closure and a zipper keep everything safe and secure.

~Cinzia

Card and Key
WALLET

FINISHED WALLET: 3" x 5"
Designed and made by Cinzia Allocca

MATERIALS

⅛ yard of teal solid for key-ring loop, snap closure, and binding
6" x 10" piece of floral print for outer wallet and zippered pocket
6" x 7" piece of coordinating green leaf print for lining pieces
3" x 5" piece of cotton batting
3"-long zipper in coordinating color*
1"-diameter metal key ring
⁷/₁₆" sew-on snap fastener

*If your zipper is longer than 3", refer to "Zipper Length" on page 43 for instructions on shortening a zipper.

CUTTING

From the floral print, cut:
1 rectangle, 3" x 5"
1 rectangle, 1½" x 4¼"
1 rectangle, 4" x 4¼"

From the green leaf print, cut:
1 rectangle, 3" x 5"
1 rectangle, 3" x 4¼"

From the teal solid, cut:
1 strip, 1½" x 25"
1 rectangle, 1½" x 3"
2 rectangles, 1½" x 2½"

MAKING THE WALLET PIECES

Use a ¼"-wide seam allowance throughout, unless otherwise noted.

1 To make the main body piece, lay the floral 3" x 5" rectangle wrong side up on your work surface. Place the batting rectangle over the floral rectangle. Lay the green leaf print 3" x 5" rectangle over the batting, right side up. Baste the layers together. Quilt as desired. The sample shown was quilted with vertical lines spaced ¼" apart.

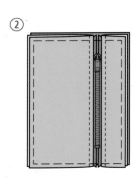

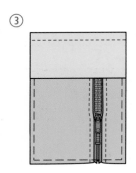

2 To make the zippered pocket, fold the floral 1½" x 4¼" and 4" x 4¼" rectangles in half lengthwise, wrong sides together; press. Place the closed zipper on your work surface with the zipper pull at the top. Lay the narrower of the two rectangles on the right side of the zipper, with the folded edge closest to the zipper teeth; pin the folded edge to the zipper tape. Using a zipper foot, edgestitch approximately ⅛" from the folded edge. Stitch the remaining rectangle to the left side of the zipper in the same manner. ①

3 With right sides up and raw edges aligned, baste the zippered pocket piece to the green leaf print 3" x 4¼" rectangle, stitching ⅛" from the edges. ②

4 Cut a 3"-long strip from the teal 1½" x 25" binding strip. Unzip the pocket zipper. With right sides together and raw edges aligned, stitch the strip to the short end of the pocket piece as shown. ③

5 Fold the binding strip over the raw edges of the pocket piece. Fold under ¼" of the long raw edge and blindstitch the folded edge to the back of the pocket. ④

6 To make the key-ring loop, press the teal 1½" x 3" rectangle in half lengthwise, wrong sides together. Open up the strip and fold the long edges toward the center crease; press again. Fold the strip in half lengthwise along the original center crease and edgestitch ⅛" from both long edges. Fold the strip in half crosswise so that the ends meet; stitch the ends together ⅛" from the raw edges.

7 To make the snap closure, place the teal 1½" x 2½" rectangles right sides together. Sew around three sides, leaving one short side open. Clip the corners and turn the piece right side out; press. Edgestitch ⅛" from the three stitched sides.

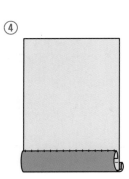

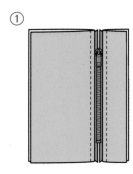

ASSEMBLING THE WALLET

1 With raw edges aligned, position the snap closure and key-ring loop on the green leaf print side of the main body piece. Baste the pieces in place. ⑤

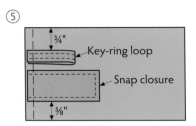

2 Place the zippered pocket, right side up, over the lining side of the main body piece, aligning the ends opposite the snap closure and key-ring loop. Baste along the long edges and short, unbound end. ⑥

3 On one end of the remainder of the teal binding strip, fold under ½"; press. With right sides together and raw edges aligned, position the folded end on the front of the wallet (pocket side) at the center of one long edge. Starting at the folded end, stitch the binding in place, stopping ¼" from the corner; backstitch and cut the threads. Remove the wallet from the machine.

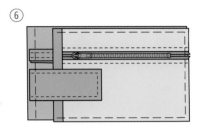

4 Fold the binding strip up to form a 45° angle at the corner. Keeping the angled fold intact, fold the binding strip back down along the next edge so that the raw edges of the binding and wallet are aligned. Start sewing at the binding edge and stop ¼" from the next corner; backstitch and cut the threads. ⑦

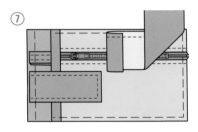

5 Repeat step 4 at each corner, stopping when you are about 1" from where you began stitching. Backstitch and remove the wallet from the machine. Fold the end of the binding strip so the fold butts up against the fold you made at the beginning. Trim the excess fabric to ½"; press. Continue stitching the binding in place, backstitching at the beginning and end. ⑧

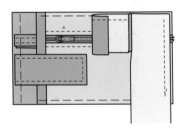

6 Fold the binding over the raw edges to the back side of the wallet (floral print side). Fold under ¼" of the binding raw edge and blind-stitch the folded edge in place.

7 Stitch one piece of the snap fastener to the underside of the snap closure piece and the other piece to the corresponding location on the zippered pocket. You'll need to unzip the pocket so you only stitch through the top layer of the pocket.

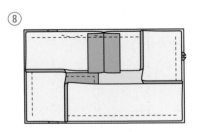

8 Slide the key ring onto the loop and your wallet is done!

Oilcloth WALLET

FINISHED WALLET: 6½" x 7¼" (open); 6½" x 3⅝" (closed)

Designed and made by April Moffatt

MATERIALS

¼ yard of 45"-wide vinyl oilcloth or laminated cotton for outer wallet

⅓ yard of 60"-wide cotton canvas or duck cloth in a coordinating solid for lining and bows

1 yard of ½"-wide double-fold bias tape in a contrasting color

½ yard of 20"-wide medium-weight fusible interfacing

Magnetic snap closure

1"-diameter metal key ring

1"-diameter button

Heavy-duty sewing thread in contrasting color for topstitching

100/16 sewing-machine needle

Fabric marking pen or pencil

CUTTING

From the fusible interfacing, cut:

2 rectangles, 7" x 7¾"

1 rectangle, 3¼" x 6⅛"

1 rectangle, 3¼" x 5½"

1 rectangle, 3¼" x 4¾"

1 rectangle, 3¼" x 4⅛"

1 rectangle, 1⅛" x 4⅛"

2 pockets (page 22)

1 tab (page 22)

From the canvas or duck cloth, cut:

1 rectangle, 7" x 7¾"

2 rectangles, 4½" x 7"

2 rectangles, 4⅛" x 4½"

1 rectangle, 3¼" x 6⅛"

1 rectangle, 3¼" x 5½"

1 rectangle, 3¼" x 4¾"

1 rectangle, 3¼" x 4⅛"

1 rectangle, 2" x 3⅜"

1 rectangle, 1⅛" x 4⅛"

2 pockets

2 tabs

From the oilcloth, cut:

1 rectangle, 7" x 7¾"

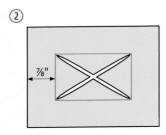

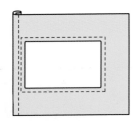

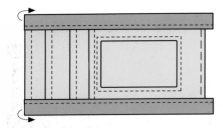

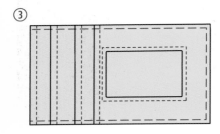

MAKING THE WALLET PIECES

Use a ¼"-wide seam allowance throughout, unless otherwise noted.

1. Fuse the interfacing pieces to their corresponding-size canvas and oilcloth pieces, following the manufacturer's instructions and using a pressing cloth to prevent the oilcloth from melting. (Note that only one of the tab pieces is interfaced.) Use the pocket pattern to round the corners of the oilcloth and canvas 7" x 7¾" rectangles.

2. To make the tab closure, refer to the pattern on page 22 to mark the position of the snap closure on the tab piece with the interfacing. Follow the manufacturer's instructions to apply the female part of the snap closure to the marked tab piece, placing the washer on the wrong side and the snap on the right side. Place the remaining tab piece right sides together with this piece and sew around the curved edges, keeping the straight edge open. Clip the curve and turn right side out; press. Topstitch ¼" from the edge. Set the tab aside.

3. To make the large pocket, cut a piece of bias tape 7" long. Place the two pocket pieces wrong sides together with the raw edges aligned. Enclose the long raw edges in the bias tape and topstitch in place. Set the pocket aside.

4. To make the key-ring loop, press the canvas 2" x 3⅜" rectangle in half lengthwise, wrong sides together. Open up the rectangle and fold the long, raw edges toward the center crease; press again. Fold the rectangle in half along the center crease to enclose the raw edges. Edgestitch ⅛" from both long edges. Wrap the rectangle around the key ring and stitch the raw edges together. Set the key-ring loop aside. ①

5. To make the ID pocket and card slot section, mark ⅞" from each side of the canvas 3¼" x 4⅛" rectangle. Cut an X in the *inner marked rectangle* from corner to corner, cutting up to but not through the corners. Turn the cut edges to the wrong side of the rectangle and edgestitch ⅛" from the opening edges. Trim away the excess fabric on the wrong side of the opening. Fold under ¼" twice along one short end of the pocket and topstitch. Set the ID pocket aside. ②

6. Fold under ¼" twice along one short end of the canvas 3¼" x 4¾", 3¼" x 5½", and 3¼" x 6⅛" rectangles and topstitch a scant ¼" from the folds. With the raw edges aligned, layer the rectangles on top of each other from longest to shortest. Lay the ID pocket on top of the shortest rectangle, aligning the raw edges. Baste the pieces together along the raw edges. Wrap the long raw edges in a strip of bias tape the length of the long raw edges plus ½". Stitch in place, turning under the end of the bias tape at the card slot end to finish it. Set the pocket section aside. ③

7 To make the bows, layer the canvas 4½" x 7" rectangles, right sides together, and stitch around them, leaving a 2" opening at the center of one side for turning. Clip the corners and turn the piece right side out; press. Edgestitch ⅛" from the edges of the entire rectangle, closing the opening at the same time. Repeat with the canvas 4⅛" x 4½" rectangles. Machine baste through the center of each bow rectangle, leaving long tails at the beginning and end. Pull the bobbin thread to gather.

8 Fold under ¼" along the long edges of the canvas 1⅛" x 4⅛" rectangle and stitch in place to make the bow wrap. Center the small gathered rectangle over the large gathered rectangle and wrap the 1⅛" x 4⅛" rectangle around the bows, overlapping the ends as much as necessary to secure the bows. Hand stitch the ends to each other. Set the bows aside.

ASSEMBLING THE WALLET

1 Mark the position of the snap closure on the right side of the oilcloth 7" x 7¾" rectangle as shown. Follow the manufacturer's instructions to apply the male part of the snap closure at the marked location, placing the washer on the wrong side and the snap on the right side. ④

2 Place the canvas 7" x 7¾" rectangle on your work surface right side up. Lay the large pocket on one end, right side up with the bias-tape edge toward the center and the raw edges aligned. Position the ID and card slot pocket ½" from the large pocket as shown, aligning the raw edges on the right side. Place the key-ring loop between the two pockets on the right side of the canvas rectangle, aligning the raw edges. Center the tab over the large pocket, with the snap side down and the raw edges aligned. Baste around the outer edges. ⑤

3 Place the oilcloth rectangle over the canvas rectangle from step 2, right sides together and raw edges aligned. Using a ½"-wide seam allowance, stitch around the outer edges, leaving a 3" opening along one side for turning. Clip the corners and turn the piece right side out. Gently push out the corners; press, using a pressing cloth on the oilcloth side to prevent it from melting, and turning under the seam allowances along the opening. Topstitch ¼" from the wallet edges.

4 Fold the wallet in half, with the oilcloth side out, and secure it with the magnetic closure. Position the bows on the closure half of the wallet, shaping the large bow around the tab. When you're pleased with the position, open up the wallet and hand tack the bows in place through the oilcloth only. Stitch the button to the front of the tab over the snap closure.

④

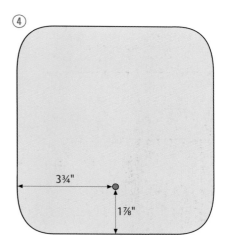

3¾"

1⅞"

⑤

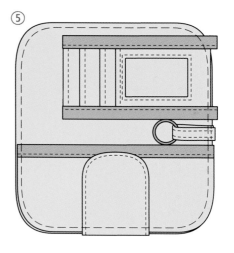

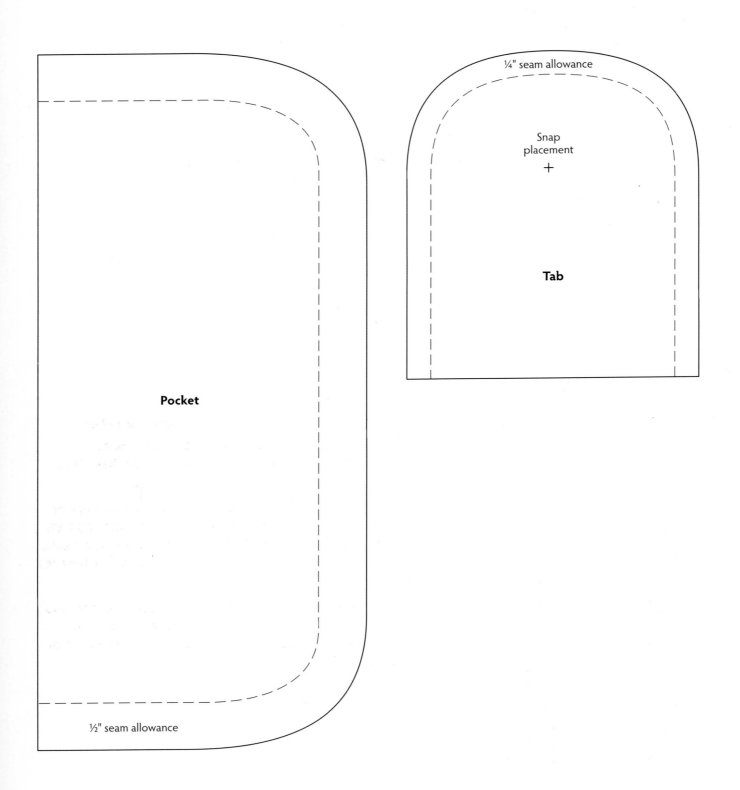

Pocket

½" seam allowance

¼" seam allowance

Snap
placement
+

Tab

Wristlet KEY HOLDER

FINISHED HOLDER: 9½" x 1¾"

Designed and made by Debbie Grifka, Esch House Quilts

MATERIALS

6" x 10½" rectangle of cotton print for front and back
2¼" x 10" rectangle of flannel for interlining
2¼" x 10" rectangle of muslin for lining
1½" of ¾"-wide Velcro
7"-long zipper to match cotton print

CUTTING

From the cotton print, cut:
1 rectangle, 2¼" x 10"
1 rectangle, ¾" x 10"
1 rectangle, 1½" x 10"
2 rectangles, 1" x 2¼"

ASSEMBLING THE KEY HOLDER

Use a ¼"-wide seam allowance throughout, unless otherwise noted.

1 To make the front, layer the muslin, flannel, and cotton print 2¼" x 10" rectangles, right sides up. Quilt as desired. Set the quilted front aside.

2 To make the zippered back, press under ¼" along one short edge of each cotton print 1" x 2¼" rectangle to make the zipper tabs. Partially unzip the zipper. Sew the pressed-under ends of each tab across the ends of the zipper, leaving 6" of zipper showing between the tabs. Trim the ends of the zipper tape to ¼". ①

3 Using a zipper foot, sew the cotton print ¾" x 10" rectangle to the top of the zipper piece from step 2. Sew the cotton print 1½" x 10" rectangle to the bottom of the zipper piece. Press the seam allowances away from the zipper piece. ②

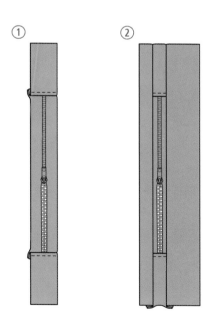

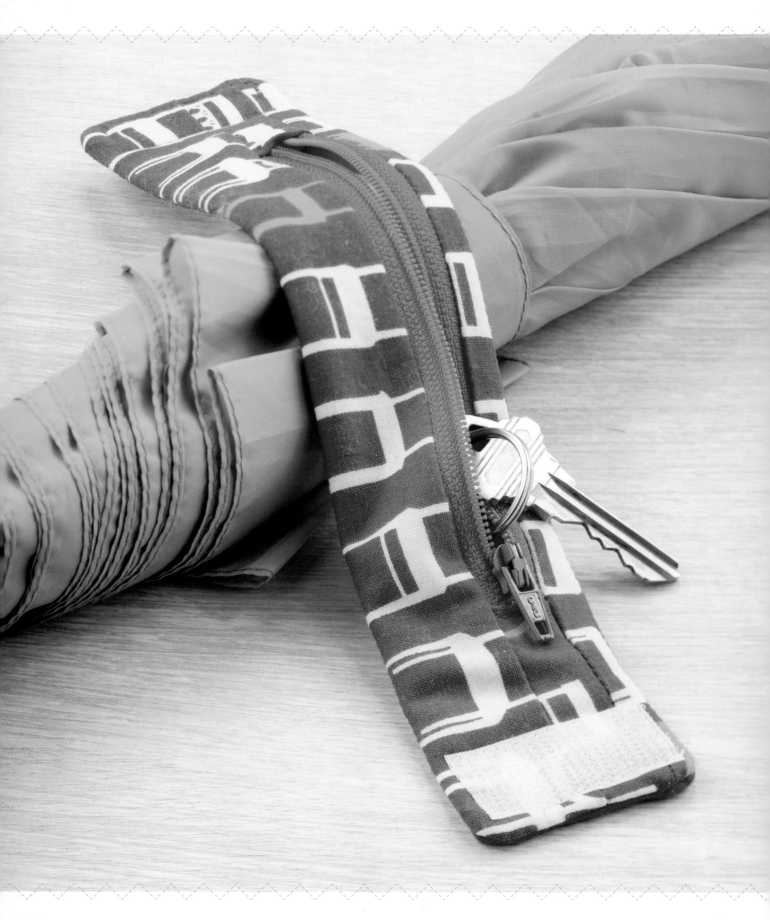

4 Make sure the zipper is unzipped at least halfway. Place the zippered piece and the quilted front piece right sides together. Sew ¼" from the edges around the entire piece, using your regular presser foot. Clip the corners. Turn the piece right side out through the zipper opening. Gently push out the corners; press.

5 Separate the Velcro. Sew one piece to the zippered back side of the key holder. Turn the piece over so the Velcro is face down. Sew the remaining piece of Velcro to the front at the opposite end. ③

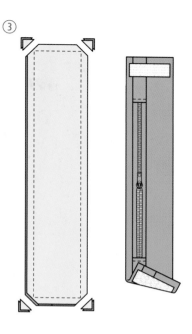

Color-Block
iPAD COVER

FINISHED COVER: 10½" x 7½"

Designed and made by Debbie Grifka, Esch House Quilts

MATERIALS

⅓ yard of blue #1 fabric for front and back
12" x 18" rectangle of fabric for lining
8¼" x 11½" rectangle of flannel for screen protector
4" x 7" rectangle of blue #2 fabric for front
3½" x 6½" rectangle of blue #3 fabric for front
2½" x 6½" rectangle of orange fabric for front
2" x 7½" rectangle of blue #4 fabric for front
2" x 3½" rectangle of blue #5 fabric for front
11" x 16" rectangle of batting
12"-long navy heavy-duty zipper

CUTTING

From blue #1 fabric, cut:
1 rectangle, 9" x 11½"
1 rectangle, 5" x 6½"

From blue #2 fabric, cut:
2 rectangles, 1" x 6½"
1 rectangle, 1" x 2"

From the lining fabric, cut:
1 rectangle, 9" x 11½"
1 rectangle, 6½" x 11"
1 rectangle, 2" x 11"

From the batting, cut:
1 rectangle, 8" x 10½"
1 rectangle, 6" x 10"
1 rectangle, 1½" x 10"

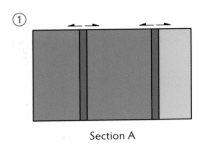

Section A

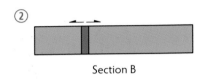

Section B

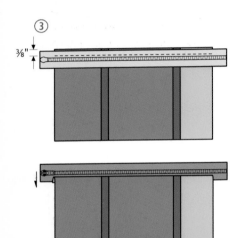

PREPARING THE FRONT AND BACK PIECES

Use a ¼"-wide seam allowance throughout, unless otherwise noted.

1 Sew the 5" x 6½" blue #1 rectangle, the 3½" x 6½" blue #3 rectangle, and the 2½" x 6½" orange rectangle together with the 1" x 6½" blue #2 rectangles as shown to make section A. Press the seam allowances away from the blue #2 rectangles. ①

2 Sew the 1" x 2" blue #2 rectangle between the blue #4 and blue #5 rectangles as shown to make section B. Press the seam allowances away from the blue #2 rectangle. ②

3 Lay the lining 6½" x 11" rectangle on your work surface, wrong side up. Center the 6" x 10" batting rectangle over the lining piece. Place section A, right side up, over the batting. Baste the layers together and quilt as desired. Trim the piece to measure 6½" x 11", if needed. Repeat the layering and quilting process with the lining 2" x 11" rectangle, 1½" x 10" batting rectangle, and section B piece. Trim the piece to measure 2" x 11", if needed.

4 With right sides together, position the zipper on the right side of section A along one long edge as shown, with the zipper pull extending past the fabric. Using a zipper foot, stitch ⅜" from the long, raw edge. Press the seam allowances away from the zipper. ③

5 Place section B over the zipper, right sides together and raw edges aligned. Be sure the blue #2 strips line up across the A and B sections. Stitch ⅜" from the long, raw edges and press the seam allowances away from the zipper. ④

6 Fold under ¼" twice along of one 11½" edge of the flannel rectangle; stitch the hem in place. Repeat with both 8¼" edges. With wrong sides up, center the flannel rectangle over the pieced front, aligning the raw edge of the flannel with the long raw edge opposite the zipper. Keeping both pieces flat, pin them together near the zipper. Turn the piece over so the right side of section A is face up. Topstitch along the zipper on the section A side of the front piece. ⑤

7 Fold the long edge of the flannel rectangle, which extended over the zipper onto section B, back onto itself toward section A. Topstitch along the zipper on the section B side of the front piece, keeping the flannel out of the stitching. Do not trim the excess zipper or edges yet.

8 For the back piece, lay the lining 9" x 11½" rectangle on your work surface, wrong side up. Center the 8" x 10½" batting rectangle over the lining piece. Place the 9" x 11½" blue #1 rectangle over the batting, right side up. Baste the layers together and quilt as desired. Trim the piece to measure 8½" x 11", if needed.

ASSEMBLING THE COVER

1 Open the zipper at least halfway. Place the front cover right sides together with the quilted back piece, aligning the raw edges. Stitch around all four sides, keeping the long, hemmed edge of the flannel free. Trim the corners. Trim the excess zipper and front cover even with the back piece. Turn the cover to the right side and gently push out the corners; press.

2 Insert the iPad into the cover so that the flannel covers and protects the screen.

④

⅜"

⑤

Assemble pieces wrong side up, and then topstitch from right side of cover.

This cute little bag can be used to hold all kinds of treasures, including sewing necessities!

~Gail

Sweet Bird
DRAWSTRING BAG

FINISHED BAG: 10" x 10"

Designed and made by Gail Pan

MATERIALS

Yardage is based on 42"-wide fabric.

⅜ yard of red floral for outer bag
⅜ yard of cream floral for lining
8" x 8" square of cream polka-dot fabric for embroidered background
3" x 7½" rectangle of red polka-dot fabric for casings
8" x 8" square of fusible woven interfacing
2 rectangles, 11" x 13", of batting
60" of ⅛"-diameter cream cord
6-strand embroidery floss in red, green, pink, and light gold
Water-soluble basting glue
Size 8 ecru pearl cotton
Size 8 or 9 embroidery needle for embroidery
Size 5 or 6 embroidery needle for quilting
Size 10 or 11 straw needle for appliqué
Fabric marking pen or pencil

CUTTING

From the red floral, cut:
2 rectangles, 10½" x 12½"

From the cream floral, cut:
2 rectangles, 10½" x 12"

From the red polka-dot fabric, cut:
2 strips, 1½" x 7½"

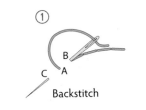

Backstitch

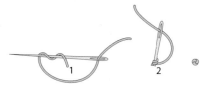

French knot

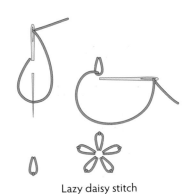

Lazy daisy stitch

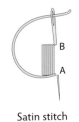

Satin stitch

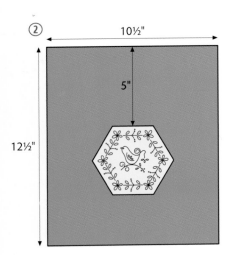

MAKING THE BAG FRONT

1 Follow the manufacturer's instructions to fuse the interfacing square to the wrong side of the cream polka-dot square. Center and trace the embroidery pattern on page 33, including the outer hexagon lines, onto the right side of the interfaced square using your preferred method.

2 Embroider the design with the size 8 or 9 embroidery needle, using the floss colors and stitches indicated on the pattern. ①

3 Cut out the finished design ¼" from the outer lines. Glue baste the stitched design to the right side of a red floral rectangle, 5" from a short edge. Apply the basting glue a little more than ¼" inside the marked line so you'll be able to turn under the seam allowance. With the size 10 or 11 straw needle and matching thread, needle-turn appliqué the design in place. ②

4 Baste the bag front to a batting rectangle. Using the pearl cotton and size 5 or 6 embroidery needle, quilt ¼" from the hexagon edges. Trim the batting even with the fabric edges.

ASSEMBLING THE BAG

Use a ¼"-wide seam allowance throughout.

1 Baste the remaining red floral rectangle to the remaining piece of batting to make the back piece. Trim the batting even with the fabric edges.

2 To make the casing strips, press under ¼" along both long edges of each red polka-dot strip. Press under ¼" along each short end, and then glue baste the hem in place.

3 Center and pin a casing strip to the bag front, 1½" down from the top raw edge. Sew ⅛" from both long edges, leaving the ends open and backstitching at the beginning and end of each line of stitching. Pull the threads to the back of the piece, tie off, and trim. Repeat to sew the remaining casing strip to the back piece.

4 Pin the bag front and back pieces right sides together. Sew down one long side, across the bottom, and up the other long side, leaving the top open.

5 Box the corners by bringing the bottom seam and side seam together; pin. Mark a line 2" from the tip of the triangle; sew across the marked line. Repeat for the remaining bottom corner. Trim the excess fabric, leaving a ¼"-wide seam allowance. Turn the piece to the right side. ③

6 To make the lining, pin the cream floral rectangles right sides together. Sew down one long side; across the bottom, leaving an opening approximately 3" long for turning; and up the other long side, leaving the top open. Box the corners in the same manner as you did for the outer bag. Do not turn the lining to the right side.

7 Place the outer bag inside the lining, right sides together, matching the side seams; pin along the top raw edge. Sew around the top edge. Turn the bag to the right side through the opening in the lining. Slip-stitch the opening closed. Push the lining into the bag and edgestitch ⅛" from the top edge.

8 Cut the cord in half to make two equal lengths. Thread one of the lengths through one casing and around and through the other. Tie the cord ends in a knot. Repeat for the remaining length, starting on the opposite side of the bag. Pull the cords to close the bag.

③

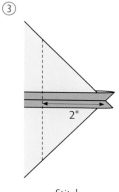

Stitch.

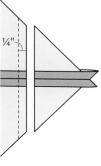

Trim.

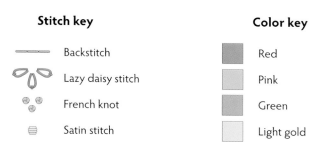

Stitch key

—— Backstitch

Lazy daisy stitch

French knot

Satin stitch

Color key

Red

Pink

Green

Light gold

Casual Crossed
HOBO BAG

FINISHED BAG: 16" x 16"

Designed and made by Missy Shepler

MATERIALS

Yardage is based on 42"-wide fabric.

½ yard *each* of 2 coordinating prints for bag, strap, ring loops, and button loop (cotton indigo, lightweight canvas, denim, or lightweight home-decor fabrics recommended)

1 yard of coordinating print for lining and interior pocket

1" x 14" strip of cotton batting

Two 1¼"-diameter metal O rings

⅝"-diameter magnetic snap or ⅞"-diameter button

Fabric marking pen or pencil

CUTTING

Enlarge the bag and interior pocket pattern on page 39 to 250% and use the enlarged patterns to cut out the bag pieces. Make sure to transfer the guide marks to each piece.

From *each* of the 2 coordinating bag fabrics, cut:

1 bag piece (2 total)

1 reversed bag piece (2 total)

1 rectangle, 2½" x 3" (2 total)

From *1* of the bag fabrics, cut:

1 strip, 2½" x 18"

1 rectangle, 1" x 6" (omit if using magnetic snap)

2 squares, 1½" x 1½" (omit if using button closure)

From the coordinating print for lining and interior pocket, cut:

2 bag pieces

2 reversed bag pieces

1 interior pocket piece

1 reversed interior pocket piece

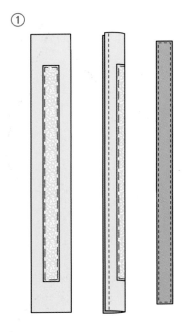

PREPARING THE STRAP

Use a ½"-wide seam allowance throughout, unless otherwise noted.

1 To make the ring loops, fold each of the bag fabric 2½" x 3" rectangles in half, right sides together, to form rectangles measuring 1¼" x 3". Using a ¼"-wide seam allowance, sew along the long, raw edges of each rectangle. Center the seams on one side and press the seam allowances open. Turn the rectangles right side out, re-center the seam, and press again. Topstitch along each long edge of both rectangles. Set the ring loops aside.

2 If using a button closure, press ¼" to the wrong side along each long edge of the bag fabric 1" x 6" rectangle. Fold the pressed strip in half lengthwise, encasing the long raw edges, and press again. Stitch down the center of the pressed strip to secure. Set the button loop aside.

3 Vertically center the batting 1" x 14" strip on the wrong side of the bag 2½" x 18" strip. (The batting will be shorter than the fabric strip at each end.) Baste the batting in place. With right sides together, fold the strip in half, forming a 1¼" x 18" strip. Using a ¼"-wide seam allowance, stitch the long, raw edges together. Turn the strip right side out to form the strap. Press, and then turn ½" to the wrong side along each end of the strap. Topstitch along the outer edge of the strap, anchoring the batting and pressed edges in place. Remove the basting stitches. Set the strap aside. ①

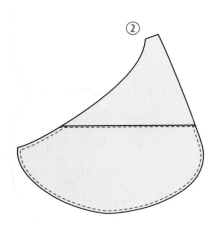

ASSEMBLING THE BAG

1 With right sides together and raw edges aligned, stitch the interior pocket and reversed interior pocket pieces together along the upper edges. Turn the pocket pieces wrong sides together, encasing the seam allowances; press. Topstitch along the upper edge.

2 With raw edges matching, align the pocket along the right side of one lining piece. Sewing within the seam allowance, sew the pocket in place along the raw edges. ②

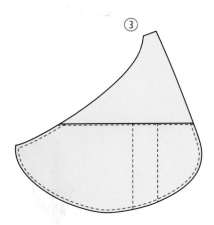

💡 Everything in Its Place

Stitch through the pocket and lining, perpendicular to the top pocket edge, to divide the pocket into smaller compartments if desired. ③

----

3 Place lining pieces (one regular and one reversed) right sides together, aligning the raw edges. Stitch between points A and B. Press the seam allowances to one side. Repeat with two matching bag pieces, pressing the seam allowances in the same direction as the lining pieces. ④

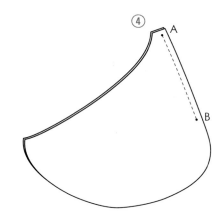

4 Wrap a ring loop through a metal ring and match the short raw edges. Place the loop against the joined lining with right sides together, aligning raw edges and centering the loop along the seam at point A. Pin, then stitch the loop in place, sewing within the seam allowance.

5 If you're using a button closure, fold the button loop in half and match the short raw edges. Place the loop against the joined lining, right sides together, at the center snap/button mark. Align the raw edges. Pin, and then stitch the loop in place, sewing within the seam allowance.

If you're using a magnetic snap, follow the manufacturer's instructions to insert one-half of the snap in place on the lining, using a bag fabric 1½" square as reinforcement on the wrong side.

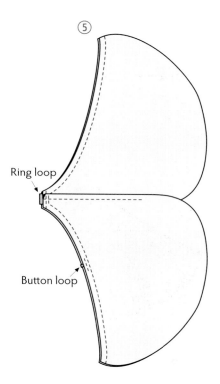

6 With right sides together, align the joined bag and joined lining pieces from step 3 along the upper edge, sandwiching the handle loop from step 4 and the button/snap closure from step 5 between the layers. Stitch the lining to the bag along the upper edge; press. ⑤

7 Fold the bag out of the way. With right sides together, realign the lining pieces, matching the raw edges along the side and lower edges. Stitch the lining pieces together from point B across the bag bottom. Press the seam allowances to one side.

8 Repeat step 7 with the bag, leaving a 3" opening in the seam for turning. Press the seam allowances to one side. Reach inside the opening and grasp the metal ring to turn the bag right side out; press, folding the seam allowances to the inside along the opening. Hand stitch the opening closed.

9 Tuck the lining inside the bag and press the upper edge of the bag. Topstitch along the upper edge and the base of the ring loop.

10 Repeat steps 3–9 to make the other half of the bag, eliminating the button loop if you're using a button closure.

11 Tuck the bag side with the pocket inside the other half of the bag, aligning side and bottom seams and center snap/button markings. Pin the two bag sides together. Topstitch on each side of the bag side seam, all around the outer perimeter of the bag.

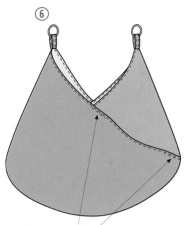

Stitch bag together at
outer pocket openings.

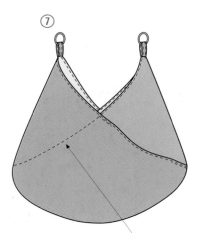

Stitch bag sides together
using inner bag as guide.

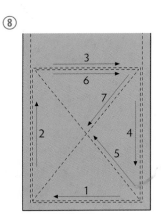

12 Following the upper edge topstitching, stitch the bag sides together at the top and bottom edges of the outer pocket openings. ⑥

13 Using the upper edge of the inner bag as a guide, stitch the bag sides together along the inner bag edge to secure the outer pockets. If you prefer that the line not show, hand stitch this seam. ⑦

FINISHING THE BAG

1 Loop one end of the bag strap through each of the metal rings, overlapping the end onto itself approximately 1½". Box stitch the folded ends to secure the handle in place. ⑧

2 If using a button closure, sew the button in place at the corresponding location at the center front.

💡 Button Buddies

Place a second, smaller button inside the bag directly behind the large outer button, and sew through both buttons to secure them in place. Knot and wrap the thread ends around the smaller button base. The smaller button reinforces the outer button, and hides your stitches.

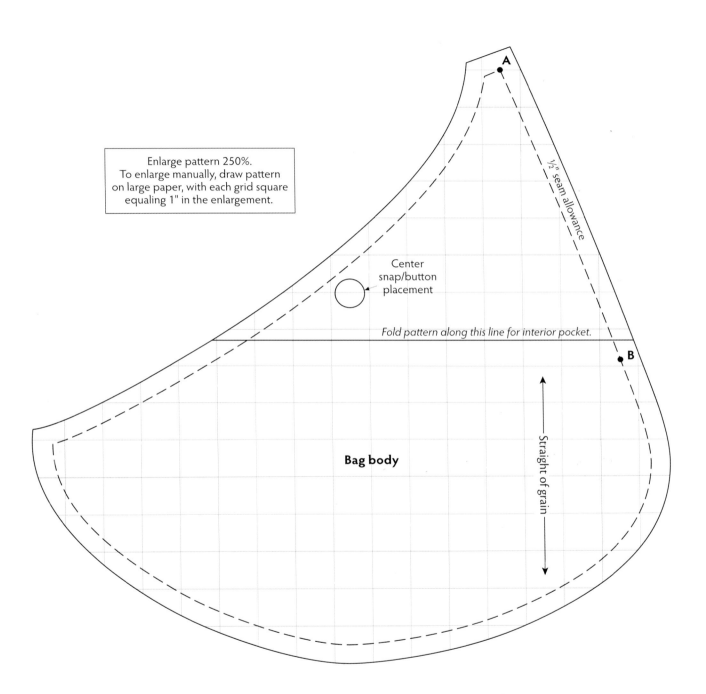

Enlarge pattern 250%.
To enlarge manually, draw pattern on large paper, with each grid square equaling 1" in the enlargement.

A

½" seam allowance

Center snap/button placement

Fold pattern along this line for interior pocket.

B

Bag body

Straight of grain

Pieced Kimono
SCARF

FINISHED SCARF: 11" x 56", excluding fringe
Designed and made by Linda Turner Griepentrog

MATERIALS

Yardage is based on 42"-wide fabric.

16 rectangles, 4" x 8", of assorted vintage kimono fabrics for pieced center section
1 yard of black silk dupioni for backing and borders
¾ yard of 6"-long rayon chainette fringe*

If you can't find chainette fringe at your local fabric store, it's available from VogueFabricsStore.com.

CUTTING

From the *lengthwise grain* of the black silk dupioni, cut:
2 rectangles, 15½" x 30"

ASSEMBLING THE SCARF

Use a ¼"-wide seam allowance throughout.

1 To make the pieced center section, lay out the assorted fabric rectangles end to end in a pleasing arrangement of two horizontal rows of eight rectangles each. Sew the rectangles in each row together. Press the seam allowances in one direction. ①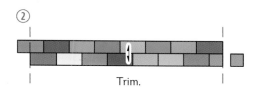

2 Shift the bottom row half a rectangle to the right. Sew the rows together. Press the seam allowances open. Trim the ends even. ②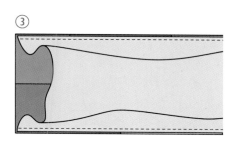

3 Sew the short ends of the black silk rectangles together. Press the seam allowances open.

4 With right sides together, align one short end of the pieced silk rectangle with one short end of the pieced center rectangle from step 2. Stitch the pieces together along the long edges, noting that the silk rectangle is larger than the center section and will not lie flat. Press the seam allowances toward the center section. ③

Trim.

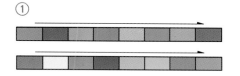

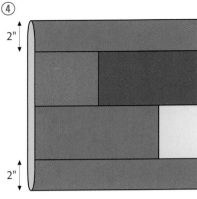

④

2"

2"

5 Turn the scarf right side out and press so that a 2"-wide black silk border is formed along both long sides. Square and trim the ends, if necessary. ④

6 Press under ¼" of the open scarf ends to the wrong side.

7 Cut a 12" length of fringe and turn under the ends ½". Pin the fringe between the pressed scarf ends so that the fringe header is enclosed. ⑤

8 Hand stitch the fringe on both ends of the scarf, stitching on both the front and back of the scarf.

9 Press the finished scarf.

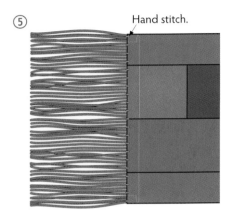

⑤   Hand stitch.

💡 Vintage Variations

Old kimono fabrics sometimes have imperfections, stains or worn spots, so try to work around those when cutting rectangles. If fabrics are thin and tend to shift while cutting, spray them with a starch alternative to add stability.

💡 Zipper Length

If your zipper is longer than 16", you can shorten it by creating a new bottom stop. Simply stitch over the coils a few times 16" from the top stop. Then cut off the end of the zipper about ½" below the new stop. If your zipper is shorter than 16", you can add a longer zipper tab (see "Zipper Tabs" on page 45).

Triangular
KNITTING NEEDLE CASE

FINISHED CASE: 3" x 17½"

Designed and made by Josée Carrier

MATERIALS

Yardage is based on 42"-wide fabric.

½ yard of print fabric for patchwork strip, case ends, and lining
2½" x 6" rectangle *each* of blue, orange, and green solids for patchwork strip
¼ yard of light-gray solid for outer case background
1 fat quarter (18" x 21") of dark-gray solid for binding
12" x 28" piece of batting
16"-long nylon zipper in coordinating color
¾" bias-tape maker (optional)
Fabric marking pen or pencil

CUTTING

From the light-gray solid, cut:
2 strips, 1½" x 17½"
1 strip, 5½" x 17½"
2 rectangles, 1" x 2"*

From the print fabric, cut:
2 rectangles, 1½" x 5½"
1 rectangle, 14" x 22"
1 rectangle, 6" x 10"
1 rectangle, 10" x 14"

From *each* of the blue, orange, and green solids, cut:
4 rectangles, 1½" x 2½" (12 total)

From the *bias* of the dark-gray solid, cut:
4 strips, 1⅜" x at least 20"

From the batting, cut:
1 rectangle, 12" x 20"
1 rectangle, 8" x 12"

These pieces are for the zipper tabs; you may need to adjust them if your zipper is shorter than 16". See "Zipper Tabs" on page 45.

💡 Zipper Tabs

The width of the fabric pieces used to create the tabs (1") corresponds to the zipper width. You might need to adjust the length of those pieces if your zipper is not exactly 16" from the top stop to the bottom stop. Here's how to calculate the required length:

$$17\tfrac{1}{2}" - zipper\ length = \_\_\_\_\_$$
$$\div\ 2 = \_\_\_\_\_$$
$$+\ \tfrac{1}{4}" = \_\_\_\_\_ \times 2 = length\ of\ tab$$

For instance, if your zipper is 14" long, you'd need to cut your tabs 1" x 4" ([17½ – 14 = 3½ ÷ 2 + ¼ = 2] x 2 = 4).

MAKING THE CASE PIECES

1 To make the patchwork strips for the case sides and bottom, sew one print 1½" x 5½" rectangle and two blue, two orange, and two green 1½" x 2½" rectangles together as shown. Press the seam allowances toward the blue rectangles. Repeat to make a total of two patchwork strips. ①

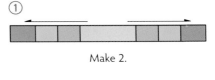

Make 2.

2 Sew a light-gray 1½" x 17½" strip to each patchwork strip. Press the seam allowances toward the light-gray strips. ②

3 Sew each unit from step 2 to a long edge of the light-gray 5½" x 17½" rectangle as shown. Press the seam allowances toward the light-gray rectangle. ③

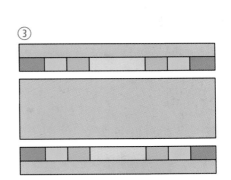

4 Lay the print 14" x 22" rectangle wrong side up on your work surface. Place the 12" x 20" batting rectangle on top of it, and then layer the pieced outer unit from step 3 right side up over the batting; baste the layers together. With the pieced outer unit on top, quilt as desired. Trim the batting and backing even with the outer unit.

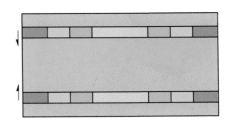

5 To make the case ends, using the pattern on page 47, trace two triangles onto the right side of the print 6" x 10" rectangle. Transfer the guide marks to each triangle.

6 Lay the print 10" x 14" rectangle wrong side up on your work surface. Place the 8" x 12" batting rectangle on top of it, and then layer the marked rectangle from step 5 right side up over the batting; baste the layers together. Quilt as desired inside both triangle shapes.

7 Cut out the triangles from the quilted piece, following the traced lines.

ASSEMBLING THE CASE

1 Following the manufacturer's instructions, use the bias-tape maker to make bias tape from the four dark-gray bias strips. If you don't have a bias-tape maker, press each strip in half lengthwise, wrong sides together. Open up each strip and fold the long, raw edges in to meet the center crease. Fold each strip in half lengthwise along the original center crease and press.

2 Fold under ¼" along the short ends of each light-gray 1" x 2" rectangle; press. Then, press the rectangles in half, wrong sides together, aligning the folded edges. Insert a zipper end into a folded rectangle. The tab's folded edges should be next to the zipper stop. If the zipper-tape extension is too long to fit in the tab, shorten it. Pin the tab in place and edge-stitch ⅛" from the fold. Repeat on the other end of the zipper. You should now have a zipper with tabs that measures the same length as the case side piece (17½").

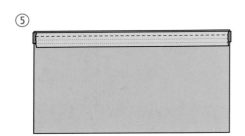

3 Place the case body on a flat surface with the print side (lining) face up. Place the zipper right side up on top of this piece, aligning the long edges as shown; baste in place. ④

4 Unfold one dark-gray bias-tape strip. Right sides together, align the long edges with the zipper and case body raw edges. Pin the tape in place, and then stitch in the crease closest to the raw edges. ⑤

5 Trim the bias-tape ends even with the sides of the quilted rectangle. Remove the basting stitches. Fold the bias tape to the right side, refold the raw edge under along the crease line, and hand stitch the bias-tape folded edge to the right side of the case using a whipstitch or slip stitch.

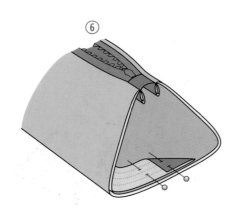

6 Repeat steps 3–5 to attach the remaining long edge of the zipper to the case body. When you're finished, you should have an open tube. Open the zipper and turn the tube wrong side out through the zipper opening.

7 Unfold a bias-tape strip and place it right sides together with the outer case on one end of the tube, aligning the raw edges. Position the tape end at the bottom of the case. Fold down the tape end at a 45° angle so the short end of the tape is also aligned with the case raw edge; pin in place. ⑥

8 Sew the bias tape in place along the crease closest to the raw edges. When you reach the zipper and the bound edges on each side of it, fold both bound edges toward the zipper. Hold them over the zipper tab while you sew the bias tape on top. When you get to where you started, continue to overlap your tape and sew about ½" past the folded end; backstitch. Trim away the excess bias tape.

9 Repeat steps 7 and 8 on the opposite end of the tube. Turn the tube right side out.

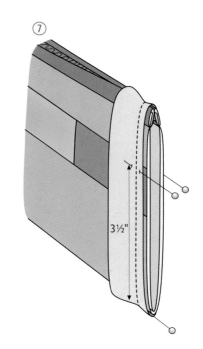

10 Lay the tube flat with the zipper centered at the top fold. Pin-mark the bottom fold at each end of the case. This pin will correspond to the mark in the middle of the triangle pieces' bottom edge. Position pins 3½" from the bottom pins on each side and each end of the case. These pins will correspond to the guide marks on the sides of the triangle pieces. ⑦

11 Place one of the quilted triangle pieces at one end of the tube. The point of the triangle with a guide mark line corresponds to the top of the case and must be aligned with the zipper. Then align the triangle sides and bottom guide marks with the pins you placed in step 10. Pin the triangle in place. ⑧

12 Baste the case and triangle together, starting at a pin and stitching all the way around. When you reach each triangle tip, position the case to make a rounded corner as shown by a dashed line on the pattern.

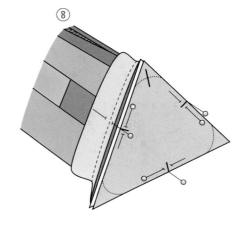

13 Sew the case and triangle together in the bias-tape seam allowance just next to the binding seam. Clip the triangle tips of the side pieces to follow the case's rounded corners.

14 Remove the basting stitches. Refold the bias tape to enclose the raw edges at the ends of the case. Hand stitch the folded edge in place to the end triangle using a slip stitch or whipstitch.

15 Repeat steps 11–14 on the opposite end of the case.

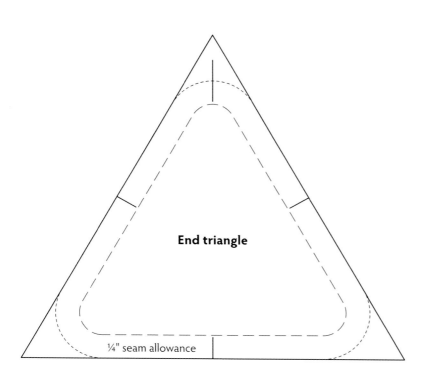

End triangle

¼" seam allowance

Artist's SKETCHBOOK COVER & PENCIL POUCH

FINISHED SKETCHBOOK COVER: Fits a 5½" x 8½" sketchbook with a ¾" spine

FINISHED PENCIL POUCH: 9" x 4¾"

Designed and made by Adrienne Smitke

Get inspired with this colorful sketchbook cover and pencil pouch! This set makes the perfect gift for your favorite artist, and can easily be customized with the recipient's favorite color palette. Both projects are great for using up those small, colorful scraps you can't bear to part with, and the sketchbook cover fits a standard-size hardcover sketchbook available at most stores or online.

~ Adrienne

MATERIALS

Yardage is based on 42"-wide fabric.

½ yard of gray print for sketchbook cover and pencil pouch

1 fat quarter (18" x 21") of orange solid for linings

3" x 12" rectangle *each* of 5 pairs of coordinating print fabrics for sketchbook cover and pencil pouch (label the first pair 1 and 2, the second pair 3 and 4, etc.)

2" x 10" rectangle of wood-grain print for pencil pouch

⅝ yard of 20"-wide lightweight fusible interfacing

9"-long zipper in coordinating color

Erasable fabric marker

CUTTING

From *each* of fabrics 1 and 2, cut:

1 strip, 1" x 12"; crosscut into:
    1 rectangle, 1" x 6¼" (sketchbook cover)
    1 rectangle, 1" x 2½" (sketchbook cover)
    1 rectangle, 1" x 1½" (pencil pouch)
1 rectangle, 1½" x 3" (pencil pouch)

From *each* of fabrics 3 and 4, cut:

1 strip, 1" x 12"; crosscut into:
    1 rectangle, 1" x 7¾" (sketchbook cover)
    1 rectangle, 1" x 2½" (sketchbook cover)
    1 rectangle, 1" x 1½" (pencil pouch)
1 rectangle, 1½" x 3" (pencil pouch)

From *each* of fabrics 5 and 6, cut:

1 strip, 1" x 12"; crosscut into:
    1 rectangle, 1" x 6½" (sketchbook cover)
    1 rectangle, 1" x 2½" (sketchbook cover)
    1 rectangle, 1" x 1½" (pencil pouch)
1 rectangle, 1½" x 3" (pencil pouch)

Continued on page 50

From *each* of fabrics 7 and 8, cut:
1 strip, 1" x 12"; crosscut into:
  1 rectangle, 1" x 7" (sketchbook cover)
  1 rectangle, 1" x 2½" (sketchbook cover)
  1 rectangle, 1" x 1½" (pencil pouch)
1 rectangle, 1½" x 3" (pencil pouch)

From *each* of fabrics 9 and 10, cut:
1 strip, 1" x 12"; crosscut into:
  1 rectangle, 1" x 6¼" (sketchbook cover)
  1 rectangle, 1" x 2½" (sketchbook cover)
  1 rectangle, 1" x 1½" (pencil pouch)*
1 rectangle, 1½" x 3" (pencil pouch)*

From the gray print, cut:
3 strips, 1" x 42"; crosscut into:
  4 strips, 1" x 19¼" (sketchbook cover)
  10 squares, 1" x 1" (sketchbook cover)
4 strips, 1½" x 42"; crosscut into:
  1 strip, 1½" x 9½" (pencil pouch)
  1 strip, 1½" x 10" (sketchbook cover)
  1 strip, 1½" x 10¾" (sketchbook cover)
  1 strip, 1½" x 11¼" (sketchbook cover)
  2 strips, 1½" x 11½" (sketchbook cover)
  18 rectangles, 1½" x 2½" (pencil pouch)
2 strips, 2" x 19¼" (sketchbook cover)
1 rectangle, 5¼" x 9½" (pencil pouch)

From the orange solid, cut:
1 rectangle, 10½" x 19¼" (sketchbook cover)
2 rectangles, 5¼" x 9½" (pencil pouch)

From the wood-grain print, cut:
9 rectangles, 1" x 1½" (pencil pouch)

From the lightweight fusible interfacing, cut:
1 rectangle, 10½" x 19¼" (sketchbook cover)
2 rectangles, 5¼" x 9½" (pencil pouch)

*You can choose either fabric 9 or 10 for these pieces;
you don't need to cut both.*

PIECING THE SKETCHBOOK COVER FRONT

Use a ¼"-wide seam allowance throughout, unless otherwise noted.

1 Sew the 1" x 2½" rectangles of fabrics 1–10 together into pairs as determined earlier. Press the seam allowances toward the darker fabric. ①

2 Draw a diagonal line from corner to corner on the wrong side of each gray print 1" square.

①
Fabrics 1
and 2

Fabrics 3
and 4

Fabrics 5
and 6

Fabrics 7
and 8

Fabrics 9
and 10

3 Place a marked square right sides together with one end of the remaining fabric 1 sketchbook cover strip as shown. Sew on the marked line. Trim ¼" from the stitching line. Press the seam allowances toward the resulting triangle. Repeat with the remaining sketchbook cover strips of fabrics 3, 5, 7, and 9. ②

4 Repeat step 3 with the remaining sketchbook cover strips of fabrics 2, 4, 6, 8, and 10, placing the marked gray squares on the strips with the marked line positioned as shown. ③

5 Sew the fabric 1 and 2 strips from steps 3 and 4 together along their long edges as shown. Press the seam allowances toward the darker fabric. Repeat with the remaining strips from steps 3 and 4, matching strips of the same length into color pairs as determined earlier. ④

6 Match each of the units from step 5 with the appropriate gray print 1½"-wide strip and a matching unit from step 1 as shown and sew them together. Press the seam allowances toward the gray print. Your strips should finish to 19¼" long. ⑤

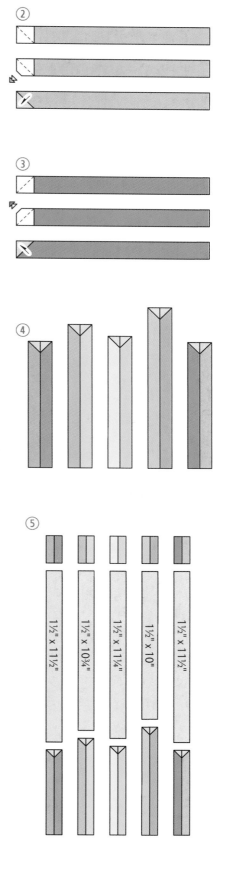

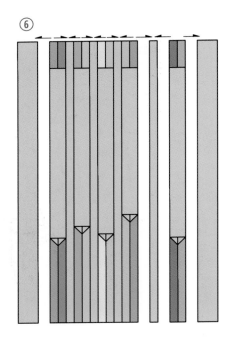

⑥

⑦ Alternately sew the pieced strips from step 6 and the gray print 1" x 19¼" strips together. Sew the gray print 2" x 19¼" strips to the sides of this unit. Press the seam allowances toward the gray print strips. ⑥

ASSEMBLING THE SKETCHBOOK COVER

1 Follow the manufacturer's instructions to fuse the interfacing to the wrong side of the orange solid 10½" x 19¼" lining rectangle.

2 Pin the lining and the pieced sketchbook cover right sides together. Starting on one of the long edges and using a ½"-wide seam allowance, stitch all the way around the cover, backstitching at the beginning and end and leaving a 4" opening along the bottom edge. ⑦

3 Clip the corners and turn the cover right side out through the opening. Roll the edges of the seams toward the lining, and then press the cover. Topstitch along both short sides of the cover.

4 Fold the cover around the outside of your sketchbook so that it's centered over the spine and each short end wraps around the inside of the sketchbook's front and back covers equally to make the flaps. Adjust the flaps by narrowing them about ⅛" toward the outside (to allow for easing so the cover will be easier to put on your sketchbook) and then pin-mark their placement along the fold. Remove the sketchbook and then repin the cover flaps in place along the top and bottom edges of the cover. Edge-stitch ⅛" from the edges along the top and bottom of the cover, securing the flaps and closing the opening along the bottom edge. ⑧

⑦

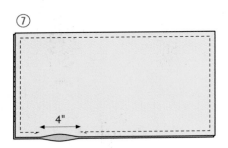

4"

⑧

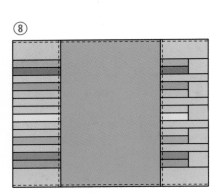

Topstitch top and bottom edges.

PIECING THE PENCIL POUCH PENCIL UNIT

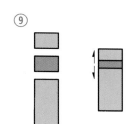

1 Sew the 1" x 1½" and 1½" x 3" rectangles of fabric 1 to a wood-grain print 1" x 1½" rectangle as shown. Press the seam allowances toward the fabric 1 rectangles. ⑨

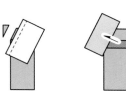

2 Using the erasable fabric marker, mark the pieced unit from step 1 as shown. Place a gray print 1½" x 2½" rectangle wrong sides together on top of the unit so that one of its long edges lines up with, and is roughly centered over, the marked lines. Don't worry about making this too perfect; the pencils will have a little bit of a "wonky" effect. Stitch the rectangle in place ¼" from the long edge, and trim the excess fabric. Press the seam allowances toward the gray print. ⑩

3 Repeat step 2 on the opposite upper corner of the step 1 rectangle so that the second rectangle overlaps the first. Trim the gray print corners even with the sides of the unit. Trim the top so that the unit measures 4¼" long. ⑪

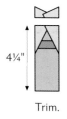

4 Repeat steps 1–3 with the remaining eight colors to make a total of nine pencil units.

Trim.

5 Sew the pencil units together in the desired order. Press the seam allowances in one direction. Sew a gray print 1½" x 9½" strip to the top of this unit. Press the seam allowances toward the strip. ⑫

4¼"

Trim.

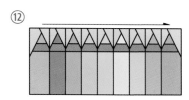

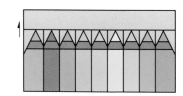

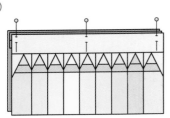

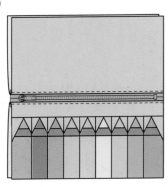

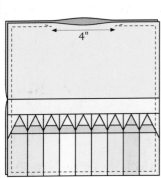

Topstitch.

ASSEMBLING THE PENCIL POUCH

1 Follow the manufacturer's instructions to fuse the interfacing 5¼" x 9½" rectangles to the wrong side of each orange solid 5¼" x 9½" lining rectangle.

2 With right sides up, align the zipper along the long edge of an orange solid 5¼" x 9½" rectangle. Align the pieced pencil unit, wrong side up, over the zipper and lining; pin all three layers in place. ⑬

3 Using a zipper foot and a ¼"-wide seam allowance, sew through all the layers, backstitching at the beginning and end. Move the zipper pull as needed to make stitching along the zipper easier. Press the seam allowances away from the zipper using low heat and the point of your iron.

4 Repeat steps 2 and 3 to sew the remaining orange solid and gray print 5¼" x 9½" rectangles to the opposite side of the zipper.

5 With the unit flat and a lining rectangle behind the front and back pieces, topstitch along the seam on both sides of the zipper. ⑭

6 Unzip the zipper halfway. Match the outer pieces of the pouch right sides together, and then match the lining pieces right sides together. Align the raw edges and let the zipper tape fold over itself at each end with the zipper teeth toward the outer fabric. Pin the fabrics in place.

7 Starting along the bottom edge of the lining, sew around the entire perimeter of the pouch, backstitching at the beginning and end, and leaving a 4" opening in the lining for turning. ⑮

8 Clip the corners of the pouch, being careful not to cut the stitching. Pull the bag right side out through the opening in the lining and the open zipper. Using matching thread, hand stitch the opening closed, and then push the lining inside the bag. Now you're ready to fill your pouch with art supplies and fill your newly covered sketchbook with ideas!

I designed this set while planning a trip with my sister to Turkey, where backgammon is practically a national pastime. Both of us struggled to pack light for our 17-day trip, but this board hardly added an ounce to our luggage and was durable enough to withstand being crammed in among guidebooks and souvenirs. Even if you've never played before, backgammon is easy to learn and has plenty of strategy to keep you interested. This travel set is the perfect size for stuffing in your bag, whether you're backpacking around Europe or just headed out for a picnic in the park.

~Adrienne

Travel
BACKGAMMON SET

FINISHED GAME BOARD: 9" x 12"
FINISHED POUCH: 5" x 4" (closed)
Designed and made by Adrienne Smitke

MATERIALS

Yardage is based on 42"-wide fabric, unless otherwise noted.

1 fat quarter (18" x 21") of gray felt for game board*
4" x 6" rectangle of aqua felt for game board*
4" x 6" rectangle of mustard felt for game board*
1 fat quarter of taupe solid cotton for game board and pouch
½ yard of mustard print cotton for game board, binding, game pieces, and pouch
1 fat quarter of aqua polka-dot print cotton for game pieces and pouch
30 size 20 (½"-diameter) flat-back covered button forms for game pieces
1 size 36 (⅞"-diameter) shank-back covered button form for pouch closure
1 yard of ⅜"-wide ribbon for board closure
1 set of 6-sided dice
Fabric marking pen or pencil

Both hand-dyed 100% wool felt and a rayon/wool-blend craft felt were used for the game board shown.

CUTTING

Refer to "Transferring Patterns to Felt" on page 57 to make the triangle shapes using the pattern on page 58.

From the gray felt, cut:
1 rectangle, 9" x 12"
1 rectangle, 5" x 11"
1 strip, ¾" x 9"

From the aqua felt, cut:
12 triangles

From the mustard felt, cut:
12 triangles

From the taupe solid, cut:
1 rectangle, 9" x 12"

From the mustard print, cut:
2 strips, 2" x 42"

💡 Transferring Patterns to Felt

Adrienne's favorite method for transferring patterns to felt is to trace the pattern onto the paper side of a sheet of freezer paper. Roughly cut out the shape and then iron it onto the felt (check your iron settings). Use sharp, pointy scissors to cut out the shape.

ASSEMBLING THE GAME BOARD AND PLAYING PIECES

1 Fold the gray felt 9" x 12" rectangle in half crosswise and finger-press the fold to make a crease marking the center of the rectangle. Unfold the rectangle and use the crease as a guide to center the gray felt ¾" x 9" strip on the board, and then pin it in place. Using matching thread, edge-stitch ¹/₁₆" from the long edges of the strip and then again with a scant ¹/₁₆" inside the initial stitching lines. ①

2 Alternately arrange six aqua felt triangles and six mustard felt triangles along both long edges of the game board, starting a generous ¼" from the side edges as shown and aligning the wide end of the triangle with the long edge of the rectangle. Pin the tips of each triangle in place. ②

3 Using a long basting stitch, stitch a scant ¼" from the long edges of the rectangle and across the wide ends of the triangles to tack them in place. Using matching thread and a regular stitch length, edgestitch the triangles in place, being careful that the point of each triangle stays lined up with the point of the triangle directly across from it on the board. ③

4 Layer the game board and the taupe 9" x 12" rectangle wrong sides together. Pin baste the pieces together. Cut the ribbon in half crosswise. With raw edges aligned, tack both lengths to the taupe cotton at the center of one short side. ④

5 Sew the mustard print 2" x 42" strips together end to end to make one long strip. Refer to "Binding" on page 105 to bind the game board edges using the pieced strip. Set aside the remainder of the binding strip for the pouch.

6 To make the game pieces, follow the manufacturer's instructions to cover 15 of the flat-back button forms with the mustard print and the remaining 15 flat-back button forms with the aqua polka-dot print.

①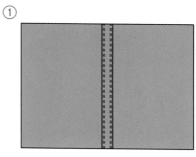

Edgestitch.

②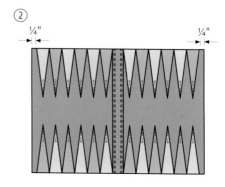

¼"　　　　　　　　　　　　¼"

③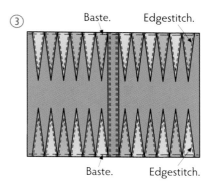

Baste.　　　　Edgestitch.

Baste.　　　　Edgestitch.

④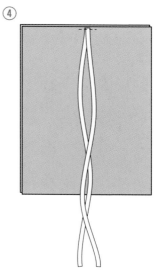

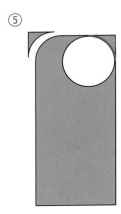

⑤

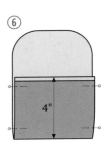

⑥

4"

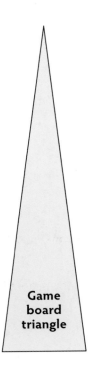

Game board triangle

Pattern is for wool appliqué and does not include seam allowances.

💡 Game Pieces

Adrienne used flat-back covered buttons for her game pieces. You can find these at your local craft or fabric store, or you can purchase them from a huge variety of shops on Etsy.com. You could also use regular buttons or stones for game pieces. You'll need 15 game pieces in each of two distinct colors.

ASSEMBLING THE POUCH

1 Using a small jar lid (Adrienne's was 3¼" diameter) as a guide, round the corners on one short end of the gray felt 5" x 11" rectangle. ⑤

2 Use the leftover binding strip to bind the untrimmed short edge of the felt rectangle. Don't worry about raw edges, they'll get hidden in the next steps—just trim the binding even with the edges of the felt.

3 Fold the bound edge up so that it creates a 4" pocket, matching the side edges. Finger-crease the fold and pin in place. ⑥

4 Fold under ½" along the one end of the remaining binding strip. Place the folded end of the binding at the folded edge of the pocket you just created. Stitch the binding in place all the way around the pouch, stopping ½" from the opposite folded edge. Trim the binding strip ½" longer than the edge of the pouch. Turn under ½" of the raw edge and finish attaching to the pouch. Fold the binding over the raw edges of the pouch and machine or hand stitch it in place to finish the edges.

5 To create the closure, cut a 1⅛" horizontal slit in the rounded pouch flap approximately 1¼" from the bound edge. Cover the shank-back button with aqua polka-dot print and sew it in place at the corresponding location on the pouch pocket.

Who says a sewing kit needs to be kept hidden in a drawer? This sweet sewing kit is pretty enough to be perched on a shelf, ready to be used when needed. A pincushion attached to the lid of the jar keeps pins and needles handy, while the jar holds all other sewing necessities. It's a great gift for anyone on your list, even a child just learning how to sew!

~Cinzia

Sewing Kit IN A JAR

FINISHED PINCUSHION: appoximately 1" high x 2½" in diameter

Designed and made by Cinzia Allocca

MATERIALS

7" x 7" square of cotton or wool fabric
Scraps of wool felt in 2 coordinating colors for flower accent
Jar with lid*
Heavy-duty upholstery thread to match or contrast with pincushion fabric
Polyester fiberfill (a large handful for each pincushion)
2- or 4-hole button (½" to ¾" in diameter)
Decorative ribbon
Size 1 milliner's needle
Fabric marking pen or pencil
Hot-glue gun
Sewing notions: thread, buttons, small scissors, seam ripper, thimble, pins, etc.

You can use any size jar. The lids of the jars shown on page 60 range from 2" to 2½" in diameter.

CUTTING

Use the patterns on page 62 to cut the following pieces.

From the square of cotton fabric, cut:
1 large circle

From the felted wool scraps, cut:
1 flower
1 small circle

MAKING THE PINCUSHION

1 Thread the needle with a 20" length of upholstery thread and make a generous knot in one end.

2 Sew a running stitch around the perimeter of the circle, about ¼" from the edge. ①

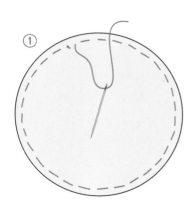

3 Pull the thread slightly to form a cupped shape, with the fabric wrong side on the inside.

4 Stuff a large handful of fiberfill into the cupped circle. Pull on the thread to close up the opening. Take a small backstitch to keep the opening closed and secure the thread. ②

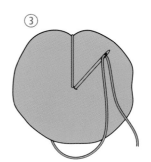

5 Push the needle up through the center of the pincushion and out the top. Keeping the thread pulled taut, wrap the thread around the pincushion and insert the needle back through the center of the pincushion and out the bottom. Be sure to always keep your thread pulled taut. Take a small backstitch to secure the thread. ③

6 Push the needle back up through the center to the top and wrap the thread around the pincushion so it crosses the previous thread and divides the pincushion into quarters. Insert the needle back through the top and out through the bottom. Secure your thread and then cut it. ④

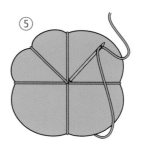

7 Cut another 20" length of upholstery thread and knot one end. Beginning at the bottom of the pincushion, push the needle up through the inside and out the center of the top. Wrap the thread around the pincushion so it goes between two of the previous wraps, and then insert the needle back through the top and out the bottom. Take a small backstitch and then insert the needle back through the inside and out the center. Wrap the thread between the remaining threads to divide the pincushion into eight segments. Insert the needle back through the top and out the bottom. Knot your thread and cut it. If gathers have formed under the threads that divide the wedges, use your fingers to smooth them out. ⑤

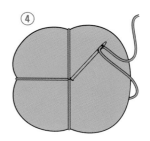

8 Cut and knot another 20" length of upholstery thread. Place the small felt circle on the felt flower. Center the flower unit on top of the pincushion. Push the needle up through the bottom of the pincushion and through the center of the flower. Place the button on the needle and then insert the needle through another hole in the button, back down through the flower, and out the bottom of the pincushion. ⑥

9 Push the needle back up through the pincushion to finish sewing the button. Once your needle is back at the bottom of the pincushion, knot and cut your thread.

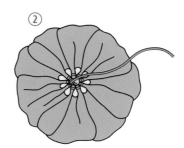

10 Using the heated glue gun, squeeze a generous amount of glue onto the lid of the jar. Press the pincushion in place and hold for a few seconds. Allow the glue to dry.

11 Tie a length of ribbon around the neck of the jar for embellishment.

12 Fill the jar with sewing notions and stick a few pins and needles into the pincushion.

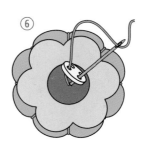

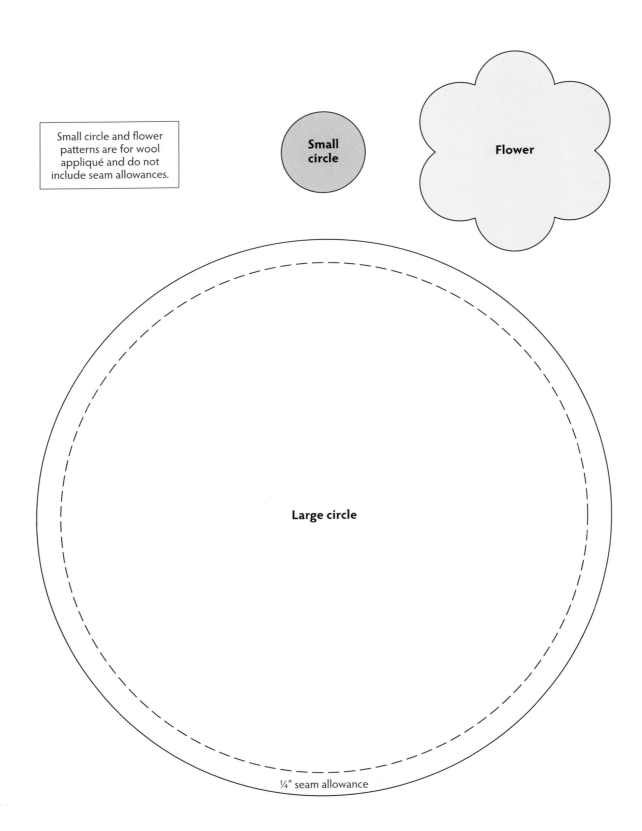

Small circle and flower patterns are for wool appliqué and do not include seam allowances.

Small circle

Flower

Large circle

¼" seam allowance

Hoot PINCUSHION

FINISHED PINCUSHION: 4" x 4¾"

Designed and made by Lesley Chaisson of Candy Corner Quilting

MATERIALS

5" x 18" rectangle of polka-dot print for body
6" x 10" rectangle of brown wool for head
5" x 10" rectangle of floral print for wings
3" x 7" rectangle of firmly woven fabric for sand pouch
1½" x 3" rectangle of cream wool for eyes
Scrap of gray felted wool for beak
2 pink ½"-diameter buttons
Pink 6-strand embroidery floss
Size 3 embroidery needle
Silica or regular sand
Polyester fiberfill
Fabric marking pen or pencil

CUTTING

Use the patterns on pages 66 and 67 to cut the following pieces.

From the floral print, cut:
2 wings
2 reversed wings

From the polka-dot print, cut:
4 pockets

From the cream wool, cut:
2 eyes

From the brown wool, cut:
2 body pieces

From the gray wool, cut:
1 beak

MAKING THE PINCUSHION

Use a ¼"-wide seam allowance throughout.

1 Place one wing and one reversed wing piece right sides together. Sew along the curved edge indicated. Repeat with the remaining wing pieces. Clip the seam allowances. Press the seam allowances in one direction and then fold the pieces wrong sides together and press again.

2 Place two pocket pieces right sides together and stitch along the top edge. Repeat with the remaining two pocket pieces. Clip the seam allowances. Press the seam allowances in one direction and then fold the pieces wrong sides together and press again.

3 Mark the dart lines on the wrong side of both body pieces. Position the eyes on the right side of one body piece where indicated on the pattern. Using a narrow zigzag stitch and matching thread, sew around each eye. Stitch the buttons to the eyes using three strands of pink embroidery floss. Place the flat beak piece below the eyes and machine stitch across the center. Fold down the top of the beak. ①

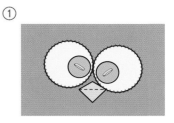

4 Place a pocket on the bottom part of the body front piece, aligning the bottom edges. Lay the wings on each side of the pocket, aligning the raw edges. ②

5 Place the remaining pocket over the wings, aligning the bottom edges. ③

6 Place the remaining body piece, right side down, over the pocket. Starting at the top of one ear and ending at the top of the other ear, stitch around the body, leaving the head open for turning. ④

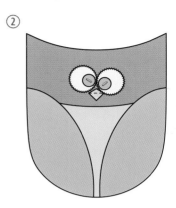

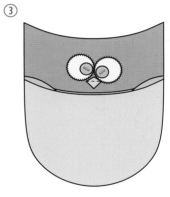

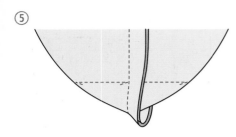

⑤

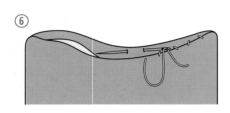

⑥

7 Bring the dart lines together on the front and back pieces and stitch along the lines, backstitching at the beginning and end of the seam. Repeat for the remaining pleat. Turn the owl right side out. ⑤

8 Fold the 3" x 7" rectangle of firmly woven fabric in half right sides together to make a piece 3" x 3½". Sew along the sides, leaving the top open. Turn right side out and fill with sand. Machine stitch across the open end, ¼" from the raw edges.

9 Place the sand pouch in the bottom of the owl, and then firmly stuff the owl with fiberfill. Turn under ¼" along the open edges and slip-stitch closed. ⑥

10 With six strands of embroidery floss, sew a running stitch along the edges of the exposed body portion of the owl.

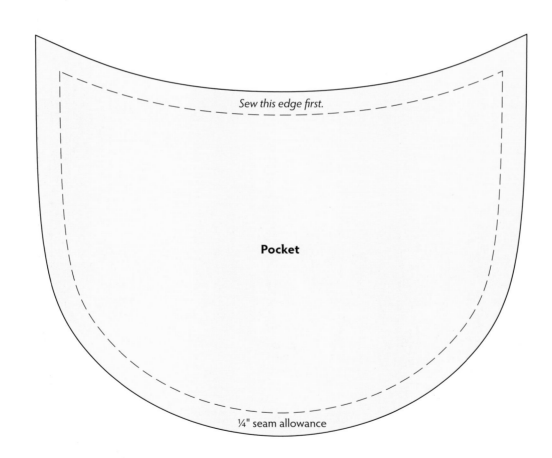

Sew this edge first.

Pocket

¼" seam allowance

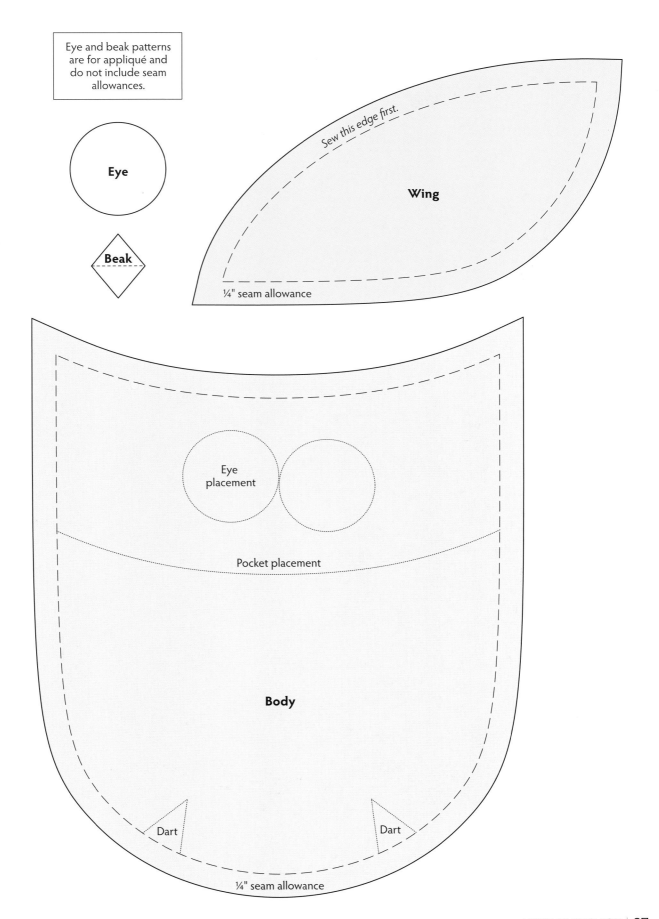

Eye and beak patterns are for appliqué and do not include seam allowances.

Eye

Beak

Wing

Sew this edge first.

¼" seam allowance

Eye placement

Pocket placement

Body

Dart

Dart

¼" seam allowance

Little Girl
BAKE SHOP SET

FINISHED APRON: 36" x 26"
FINISHED HOT PAD: 6" x 7"
FINISHED CUPCAKES: 3" x 3"
Designed and made by April Moffatt

MATERIALS
Yardage is based on 42"-wide fabric.

For the Apron

1⅓ yards of brown print for bodice and skirt
⅓ yard of green solid for neck straps, ties, and ruffle
⅛ yard of multicolored striped fabric for ruffle

For the Hot Pad

6" x 14" rectangle of brown print for front and back
⅛ yard of multicolored striped fabric for binding and hanging loop
6" x 7" rectangle of batting
1 cupcake button

For the Cupcakes

(Materials given are enough to make 2 cupcakes.)

9" x 12" rectangle *each* of bright pink, brown, white, and red wool felt
Hot pink 6-strand embroidery floss
Pink thread
Fiberfill
Fabric marking pen or pencil

CUTTING

Use the patterns on pages 73 and 74 to cut the apron bodice and cupcake pieces.

For the Apron

From the green solid, cut:
4 strips, 2½" x 16"
2 strips, 6½" x 42"

From the multicolored striped fabric, cut:
2 strips, 5½" x 42"

From the brown print, cut:
2 rectangles, 12¼" x 22"
2 bodice pieces

For the Hot Pad

From the brown print, cut:
2 rectangles, 6" x 7"

From the multicolored striped fabric, cut:
1 strip, 2" x 28"
1 rectangle, 2" x 4"

For Each Cupcake

From the brown felt, cut:
4 top pieces

From the red felt, cut:
1 cherry piece

From the white felt, cut:
1 frosting piece (cut with a scallop blade or pinking shears, if desired)

From the bright pink felt, cut:
1 side piece (cut the straight edge with a scallop blade or
    pinking shears, if desired)
1 bottom piece

MAKING THE APRON

1 To make the neck straps and waist ties, fold a green 2½" x 16" strip in half lengthwise, right sides together. Using a ¼"-wide seam allowance, stitch across one end and the long edges, leaving one end open. Turn right side out and press. Topstitch along each long edge and the finished end. Repeat with the remaining three strips.

2 To make the ruffles, sew the green 6½" x 42" strips together end to end to make one long strip. Press the seam allowances open. Press under ¼" twice along one long edge. Stitch the hem in place. Baste two lines of stitching along the long raw edge, leaving thread tails at the beginning and end. Pull the threads to ruffle the strip to approximately 34". Repeat with the multicolored 5½" x 42" strips.

3 With right sides up, pin the multicolored ruffle on top of the green ruffle, aligning the raw edges; baste together along the raw edges. Fold the ruffle in half and pin-mark the raw edge at the center.

4 Layer the brown print rectangles on top of each other and fold in half to make a piece 12¼" x 11". Refer to the illustration to mark and cut the curve as shown to shape the skirt side and lower edges. With the pieces still folded in half, pin-mark the fold at the bottom edge of each piece. ①

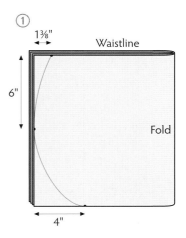

5 Unfold the skirt pieces. With right sides together and raw edges and pin-marks aligned, pin the ruffle to the bottom and sides of the skirt front. Make sure the ruffle is evenly arranged on each side. Baste the ruffle in place. Remove all of the pins except for the one marking the centers. Layer the skirt back over the skirt front, right sides together and raw edges and pin-marks aligned; pin in place. Stitch along the side and bottom edges, using a ¾"-wide seam allowance. Turn the skirt right side out; press. Topstitch ¼" from the seam line.

6 With the raw edges aligned, pin two of the straps you made in step 1 to the right side of the bodice front ¾" from the sides as shown. Baste across the upper edge of the neck straps. Baste the remaining two straps from step 1 to the sides of the bodice front ½" from the bottom edge as shown. ②

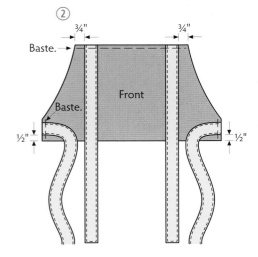

7 Place the bodice back over the bodice front, sandwiching the straps between the pieces. Using a ½"-wide seam allowance, sew the side and top edges together, leaving the waistline edge open. Clip the corners and turn the bodice right side out; press. Topstitch ¼" from the sides and top of the bodice.

8 Pin-mark the center front of the skirt and bodice along the waistline edge. With the pin-marks aligned and the fronts right sides together, use a ½"-wide seam allowance to stitch the bodice to the skirt front only. Press the remainder of the seam allowances on the front and back under ½". Pin the front and back together along the pressed-under edges. Stitch across the waistline ¼" from the pressed edge, and then stitch again ⅛" from the pressed edge.

MAKING THE HOT PAD

1 Wrong sides together, sandwich the batting rectangle between the two brown print rectangles. Baste the layers together and then quilt as desired. Square up the quilted piece if needed.

2 Refer to "Binding" on page 105 to bind the hot pad edges using the multicolored 2" x 28" strip. After you fold the strip to the back of the hot pad, machine zigzag stitch the folded edge in place or hand stitch.

3 Press under ¼" along the short ends of the striped 2" x 4" rectangle, then press under ¼" along the sides. Finally, press the piece in half lengthwise. Topstitch along the edges. Fold the piece in half to make a loop. Place the loop on one corner of the hot pad and stitch across the ends. Hand sew the button in place over the ends of the loop.

MAKING THE CUPCAKE

Use a ⅛"-wide seam allowance throughout.

1 Stitch the cupcake top pieces together in pairs, and then stitch the pairs together to make a circle.

2 Hand stitch the cherry to the center of the frosting piece. With right sides up, center and pin the frosting piece to the cupcake top. Using pink thread and decorative stitches, stitch around the frosting piece, referring to the photo as needed.

3 Stitch the darts together on the cupcake side piece.

4 Stitch the wrong side of the upper edge of the cupcake side to the right side of the cupcake top, extending the side piece just slightly beyond the edge of the top piece to allow the scalloped edge to show.

5 Stitch the side seam.

6 Turn the cupcake to the wrong side. With right sides together, stitch the cupcake bottom to the bottom of the side piece, leaving a 2" opening for turning. Turn the cupcake right side out and then stuff with fiberfill. Hand stitch the opening closed.

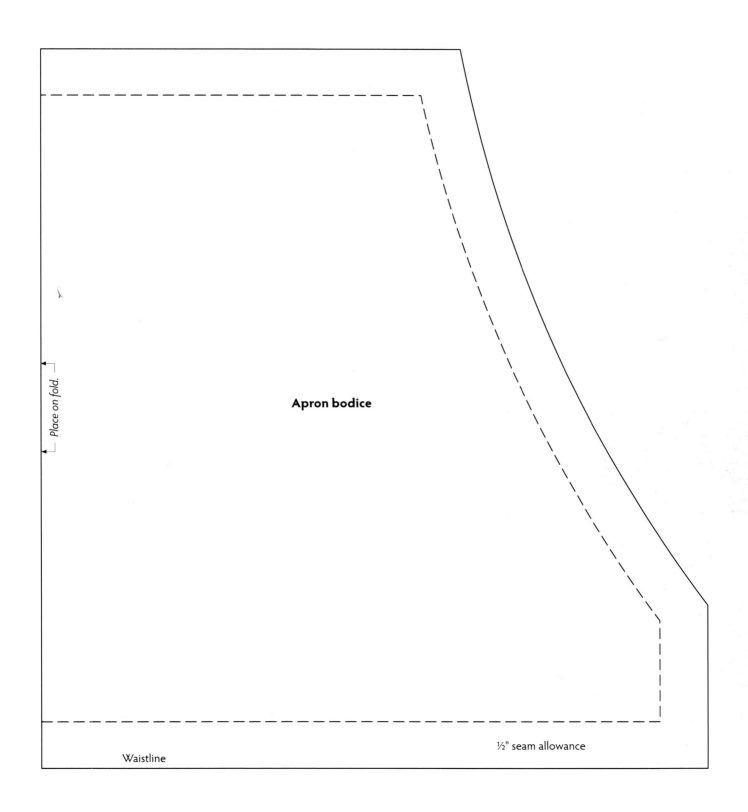

Apron bodice

Place on fold.

Waistline

½" seam allowance

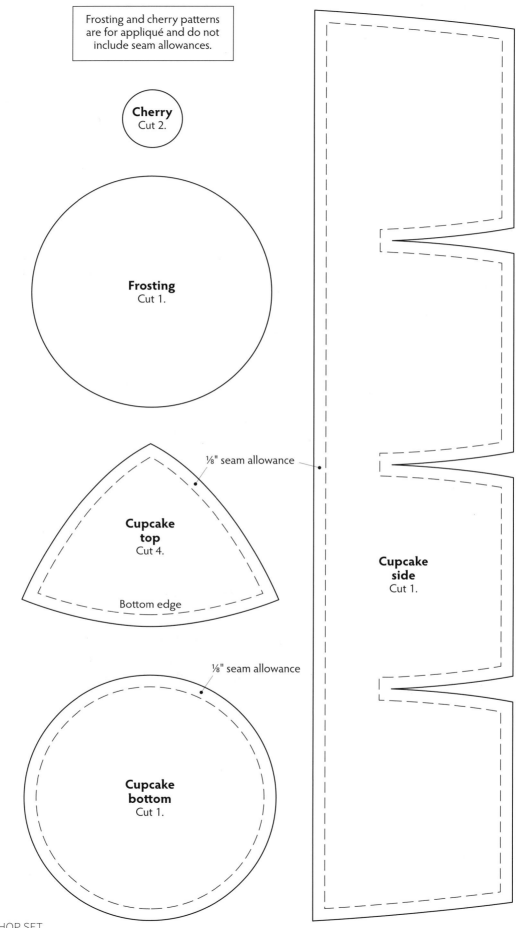

Frosting and cherry patterns
are for appliqué and do not
include seam allowances.

Cherry
Cut 2.

Frosting
Cut 1.

⅛" seam allowance

**Cupcake
top**
Cut 4.

Bottom edge

**Cupcake
side**
Cut 1.

⅛" seam allowance

**Cupcake
bottom**
Cut 1.

Holiday APRON

FINISHED APRON: 34" x 32"

Designed and made by Linda Turner Griepentrog

Let Santa know whether you've been naughty or nice by simply buttoning on this clever printed motif to the festively pieced apron bib. Use your computer to print the text on the fabric.

~Linda

MATERIALS

Yardage is based on 42"-wide fabric, unless otherwise noted.

1¼ yards of green polka-dot print for apron, neck strap, and ties
Scraps of assorted Christmas prints at least 12" long for bib and pocket
½ yard of red print for binding
8½" x 11" rectangle of fusible interfacing
1 package (2½ yards) of red jumbo rickrack
Two 1" D-rings
Two ¾"-diameter buttons
One 1"-diameter novelty holiday button
1 sheet of computer printable fabric
Fabric marking pen or pencil

CUTTING

From the green polka-dot print, cut:
1 square, 34½" x 34½"
1 rectangle, 8" x 14"
2 strips, 2½" x 30"
1 strip, 2½" x 26½"
1 rectangle, 2½" x 4"

From the *bias* of the red print, cut:
1 strip, 2" x 24"

From the assorted Christmas prints, cut:
3 or 4 various-width strips at least 12" long
9 or 10 various-width strips at least 9" long

MAKING THE NECK STRAP, TIES, AND D-RING HOLDER

Use a ¼"-wide seam allowance throughout.

1. To make the ties, fold each of the green polka-dot 2½" x 30" strips in half lengthwise, right sides together, and stitch along the long sides and across one end. Turn the ties right side out. Repeat with the green polka-dot 2½" x 26½" strip to make the neck strap.

2. To make the D-ring holder, fold the green polka-dot 2½" x 4" rectangle in half lengthwise, right sides together, and stitch along the long edges. Turn the D-ring holder right side out.

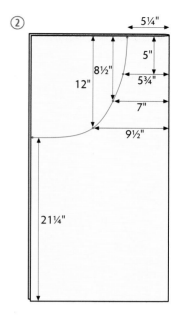

3. Edgestitch ⅛" from the edges of the ties, neck strap, and D-ring holder.

4. Thread the D-ring holder through both of the D-rings and baste the short ends together. ①

ASSEMBLING THE APRON

1. Fold the green polka-dot 34½" square in half. Refer to the illustration to cut the armhole curve in the square. ②

2. Stitch together the assorted 12" lengths of Christmas prints along the long edges to make a rectangle at least 5½" x 12". Square up the rectangle to 5½" x 12". Press the seam allowances in one direction. Press under ¼" along the rectangle lower edge. ③

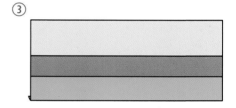

3. Lay the pieced rectangle over the front of the apron bib with the long raw edges of the pieced rectangle aligned with the bib upper edge. Cut a 12" length of rickrack and place it under the pieced rectangle lower edge so that half of the rickrack is exposed. Pin the rectangle and rickrack in place. Edgestitch the pieced overlay in place along the lower edge, securing the rickrack, and then stitch along each edge of the bib. Trim the excess pieced fabric to match the apron bib. ④

4. Press under ¼" twice along the armhole edges and topstitch the hem in place. ⑤

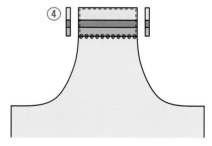

Trim.

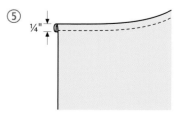

Topstitch.

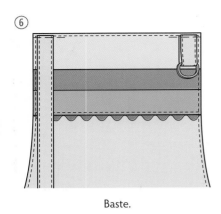

Baste.

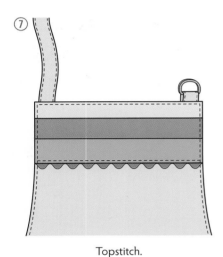

Topstitch.

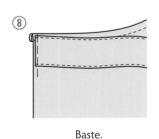

Baste.

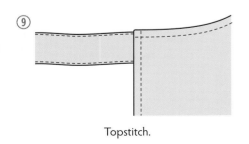

Topstitch.

5 Baste the neck strap and D-ring holder in place at the bib upper edge, matching raw edges. ⑥

6 Press under ¼" along the bib upper edge, and then press under 1¼" for the hem. Hand stitch the hem in place, being careful not to stitch through to the front. Topstitch close to the bib upper edge to secure the strap and D-ring holder in place. ⑦

7 Press under ¼" along the lower apron edge, and then press under ½" for the hem. Topstitch the hem in place.

8 Baste the ties at the lower armhole corners, matching raw edges ⑧

9 Press under ¼" twice along the apron side, and then topstitch in place, folding out the ties. ⑨

10 Piece the pocket in the same manner as the bibs area, using the assorted 9"-long strips to create an 8" x 14" rectangle. Fold the rectangle in half to create an 8" x 7" rectangle. Use the curve pattern on page 80 to mark, and then trim the lower edges opposite the fold. Repeat for the lower corners of the green polka-dot 8" x 14" rectangle.

11 Right sides together, stitch the green polka-dot pocket to the pieced pocket, leaving an opening for turning at the lower edge. Clip the corners and turn the pocket right side out; press. Hand stitch the opening closed.

12 Center and pin the pocket in place on the apron front with the lower edge 10½" above the apron hem. Cut a piece of rickrack approximately 31" long. Insert the rickrack under the pocket edge along the sides and bottom so that half of the rickrack is exposed, leaving a little extra at each end to turn under. Turn under the rickrack ends to finish and then edgestitch the pocket to the apron, backstitching at the pocket corners. ⑩

MAKING THE PRINTED SIGN

1 Using a word processing program on your computer, type the words "Naughty" and "Nice," allowing at least 3½" of space between them and 2½" margins at the top and bottom. Center the words widthwise on the lines. Select a typeface and size you like. The featured motif uses the Ravi font in 72-point size for "Nice" and 60-point size for "Naughty."

2 Following the manufacturer's instructions for ink settings and printing, print the words on the computer printable fabric. Remove the paper backing and press; treat additionally according to the instructions.

3 Fuse the interfacing to the wrong side of the printed fabric.

4 Using the sign pattern on page 80, trim the printed pieces to size, centering the words both vertically and horizontally. Place the printed pieces wrong sides together and baste ⅛" from the edges.

5 Refer to "Binding" on page 105 to bind the sign edges with the red bias strip, but leave the top edge open when you are hand stitching the binding to the opposite side of the sign. The remainder of the binding strip will be used in step 6 for the button loops.

6 Trim the excess bias strip length to 1" wide. From the strip, cut two 2" lengths. Fold the long edges in to meet in the center of the wrong side and press. Press the strips in half lengthwise. Hand stitch the folded edges closed, pulling the thread slightly to shape a loop.

7 Insert the ends of the loops under the open bias edge at the top of the sign and hand stitch in place. Finish hand stitching the bias trim to the upper sign edge, anchoring the loops in place. ⑪

8 Try on the apron and pin the sign in place at the desired location, centering it across the bib width. Mark the button locations under the loops. Sew the two functional buttons in place at the markings. Center and sew the novelty button between the functional buttons. Turn the sign to fit the appropriate mood, or wear the apron without the sign.

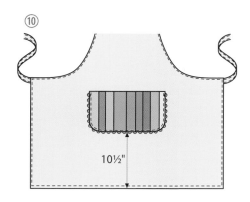

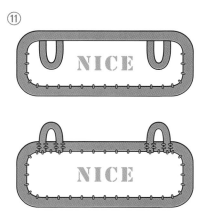

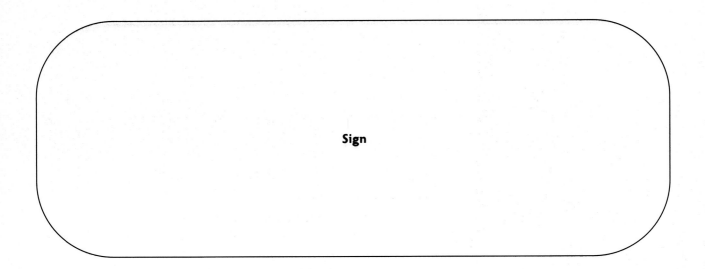

Sign

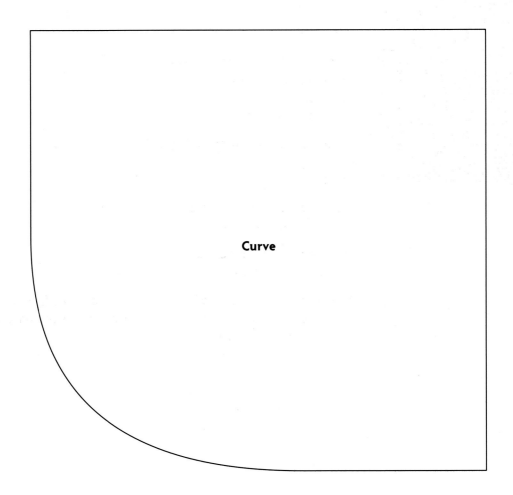

Curve

Casserole CARRIER

FINISHED COVER: Fits a 9" x 13" x 3½" pan with snap-on lid
Designed and made by Linda Turner Griepentrog

MATERIALS

Yardage is based on 42"-wide fabric.

¾ yard of cotton print for lining
⅔ yard of laminated cotton print for tote
½ yard of quilted heat-resistant insulation fabric
⅜ yard of fusible fleece
2⅛ yards of 1½"-wide webbing for handles
2 separating zippers, 24" long
Painter's tape
Spring clips

CUTTING

From the laminated cotton, cut:
2 rectangles, 11¾" x 16½"
4 strips, 2¼" x 28"
1 rectangle, 6½" x 9"

From the cotton print for lining, cut:
2 rectangles, 11¾" x 16½"
5 strips, 2½" x 28"

From the fusible fleece, cut:
2 rectangles, 11¾" x 16½"

From the insulation fabric, cut:
2 rectangles, 13" x 16"*

Check the circumference of your pan/lid in both directions. Divide each measurement by 2 and add 1" to determine the cut size if the pan differs from the featured pan size listed.

ASSEMBLING THE TOTE

Use a ¼"-wide seam allowance throughout, unless otherwise noted. Refer to "Slick Tricks" on page 85 for tips on working with laminated cottons.

1 Gently round the corners of the laminated cotton, cotton lining, and fusible fleece 11¾" x 16½" rectangles.

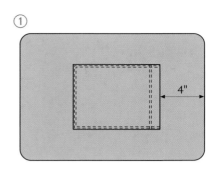

2 To make the pocket, fold under a 1" hem along one short end of the laminated cotton 6½" x 9" rectangle. Topstitch, using two rows of stitching to hold the hem in place. Turn under ¼" of the remaining three pocket sides and topstitch in place.

3 Center the pocket on the laminated cotton 11¾" x 16½" rectangle, placing the end with the wide hem 4" from the short side of the rectangle. Use painter's tape to hold it in place for stitching. Edgestitch the pocket in place along the long edges and one short end, leaving the end with the wide hem open. ①

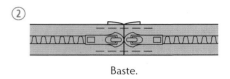

Baste.

4 Position the closed zippers end to end with the zipper pulls together and the tape ends folded under; baste across the butted edges on both sides of the pulls. ②

5 Join the laminated cotton 2¼" x 28" strips end to end, right sides together, to make one long gusset piece. Repeat with the remaining two laminated cotton strips.

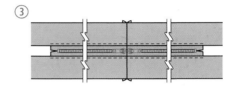

6 Fold under ¼" along one long edge of the gusset strip and place the folded edge about ¼" from the zipper teeth, lining up the gusset joining seam with the zipper joining seam. Use spring clips to clamp in place, and then edgestitch along the fold. The gusset will be longer than the zipper, so stitch only the zipper length. Repeat to stitch the remaining gusset piece to the opposite side of the zipper. ③

7 Cut the webbing into one 69" length and one 6" length. Carefully seal the webbing ends with a candle or cut them with a hot knife.

8 Mark the centers of the long edges of the laminated cotton rectangles. Position the 69"-long webbing on the rectangle *without the pocket,* butting the ends as shown. Be careful not to twist the webbing. Edgestitch the webbing sections in place, creating a box and stopping 1" from the tote body edges. Zigzag stitch the butted ends together. ④

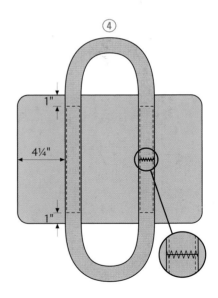

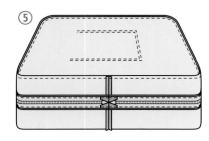

9 Matching the gusset seam to the long-edge midpoint of a laminated cotton rectangle, right sides together, clamp one gusset raw edge to the tote body, easing around the corners. Overlap the ends and trim if needed. Stitch the gusset in place. **⑤**

10 Repeat step 9 for the remaining gusset edge and tote body section. Turn the tote to the right side.

11 To create the hinge, position the 6"-long webbing over the opening between the zipper ends on the right side of the tote. Edgestitch in place, being careful as you stitch over the zipper teeth. **⑥**

ASSEMBLING THE LINING

1 Follow the manufacturer's instructions to fuse a fleece rectangle to the wrong side of each of the 11¾" x 16½" lining rectangles.

2 Join the 2½" x 28" lining strips end to end, right sides together, to make one long gusset piece. Repeat with two of the remaining lining strips.

3 Mark the center of the lining long edges. With right sides together, match the gusset seam to the midpoint; pin and stitch the gusset to the lining, turning under the gusset starting point and overlapping the gusset length at the end. Trim excess length if needed.

FINISHING

1 Slip the lining into one half of the tote, wrong sides together. Matching midpoints, loosely tack the long edges of the lining to the tote seam allowances by hand to keep it from shifting.

2 Turn under the lining gusset long edges and position them about ½" from the zipper teeth, leaving the back edges over the zipper gap extended. Clamp in place. **⑦**

3 Hand stitch the folded edges to the zipper tape, and lightly tack the extended lining edges at the tote back.

4 Repeat steps 1–3 for the second half of the tote lining, but fold under the back edge and cover the lining raw edges of the first half in the space between the zipper ends; hand stitch in place. **⑧**

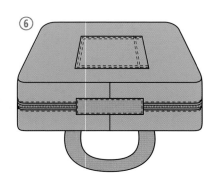

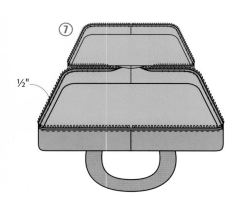

½"

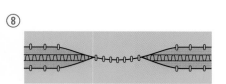

MAKING THE INSULATED SLEEVE

1 With right sides together, stitch the insulated fabric rectangles together on three sides, leaving one short end open. Zigzag or serge the seam allowances to finish the edges. Turn the sleeve right side out.

2 Refer to "Binding" on page 105 to bind the open end, using the remaining lining 2½" x 28" strip.

💡 Slick Tricks

Working with laminated cottons requires extra caution. Follow these tips for success:

» *Use a small needle (size 70/10) to avoid leaving obvious holes in the stitching lines.*

» *Avoid using pins except within the seam lines, because holes are permanent. Use clips or painter's tape to hold sections in place for stitching.*

» *Finger-press only, because an iron will damage the laminated surface.*

» *Use a Teflon or other non-stick presser foot for all topstitching. This helps the fabric feed evenly. If you don't have one, cover the under-side of your regular presser foot with painter's tape.*

Must-Have MUG RUGS

Designed and made by Pippa Eccles Armbrester

Swirly Stripes Mug Rug

FINISHED MUG RUG: 11" diameter

MATERIALS

Yardage is based on 42"-wide fabric, unless otherwise noted.

⅓ yard of solid fabric for front and binding

Scraps of assorted solid fabrics approximately 1" wide and 5" to 8" long for front

1 fat quarter (18" x 21") of print fabric for backing

13" x 13" piece of batting

Fabric marking pen or pencil

CUTTING

From the solid scraps, cut:

21 strips, approximately 1" x 5" to 8" (you may need more or fewer strips depending on their width)

From the solid fabric, cut:

1 rectangle, 8" x 11"

From the remainder of the solid fabric, cut *on the bias:*

Enough 2"-wide strips to equal 40" when sewn together end to end

ASSEMBLING THE MUG RUG TOP

1 Sew together the assorted strips along their long edges to create a rectangle that is approximately 8" x 11". If you have strips that are shorter than 8", sew these on toward the beginning and end of the rectangle. Press the seam allowances in one direction.

2 Lay the pieced rectangle and the solid rectangle next to each other, right sides up and overlapped about 3" along one of the long sides. Using a rotary cutter, very carefully cut a gently curving line along this overlap, cutting through both layers of fabric. Be careful to only cut within the 3" overlap area. If you're more comfortable marking your curve before cutting, do so. ①

① 3" overlap

3 With right sides facing, sew the curved edges of the pieced and solid rectangles together. There's no need to pin before sewing; just stitch slowly and line up the edges of the fabric as you stitch. When you're done, press the seam allowances toward the solid rectangle. ②

4 Trace a circle that is approximately 11" in diameter on the resulting piece. You can center the curving seam in the middle of the circle if you like, or place it a bit to one side. You can either create a circular template or use a compass—or search your dinner plates for one that is about the right size and use that instead! Cut along the drawn line. ③

FINISHING THE MUG RUG

1 Layer the mug rug top, batting, and backing; baste the layers together. Quilt your mug rug as desired. The one shown features free-motion machine quilting in curving lines that mirror the curve of the central seam and are about ¾" apart.

2 Refer to "Binding" on page 105 to bind the mug rug edges using the bias strips.

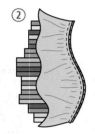

Coffee Cup Mug Rug

FINISHED MUG RUG: 10½" x 10½"

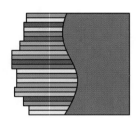

MATERIALS

Yardage is based on 42"-wide fabric.

10½" x 10½" square of white solid for background
Scraps of assorted solid fabrics for appliqués
¼ yard or 1 fat quarter (18" x 21") of dark-brown solid for binding
14" x 14" square of print fabric for backing
14" x 14" piece of batting
Template plastic
Fabric marking pen or pencil

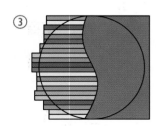

CUTTING

Use the patterns on page 90 to make templates for the circle, coffee cup, and handle appliqués from the template plastic. Lay the circle templates on the wrong side of the desired fabric and trace around them. Cut out the shapes, allowing a ¼"-wide seam allowance when cutting the large circles and a ½"-wide seam allowance when cutting out the small circles. You will use the coffee cup and handle templates later.

From the assorted scraps, cut:

8 large circles
8 small circles from different colors than the large circles
A variety of strips, approximately ¾" to 1" wide; most should be at least
    3½" long but several can be about 2" (you can also cut these as you
    piece the cup together)

From the brown solid, cut:

1 strip, 2" x 42" *OR* 2 strips, 2" x 22"

APPLIQUÉING THE MUG RUG TOP

1 To create the fabric for the cup, sew the assorted fabric strips together along the long edges until you have a rectangle that is approximately 3½" x 5". Press the seam allowances in one direction. Using the coffee cup template, trace the shape onto the pieced rectangle and cut it out along the drawn line. ④

2 Create the coffee cup handle in a similar manner, piecing together strips to create a rectangle that is approximately 2½" x 3½". Using the handle template, trace the shape onto the pieced rectangle, and cut it out along the drawn line. ⑤

3 Center the small circle template on each of the large fabric circles and trace around it. Cut out the small circle, leaving a ¼"-wide seam allowance. Clip into the seam allowance every ¼" or so (the more cuts the better for such small circles). ⑥

4 Arrange all of the appliqué pieces on the white square. Start by placing the coffee cup in the lower left. Align the handle along the left side of the cup, with the ¼"-wide seam allowances overlapping the cup so that when you've turned under the seam allowance the edges will meet exactly. Pin the appliqués in place.

5 Arrange the eight large circles in the upper right of the white square, centering a small circle underneath the opening of each large circle. Pin the appliqués in place.

6 Appliqué the coffee cup and handle to the background, turning the edges under ¼" and stitching them in place. Where the coffee cup

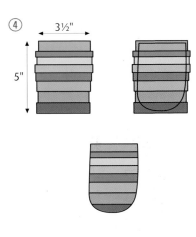

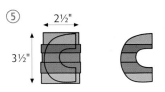

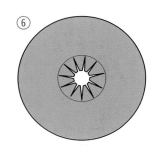

⑦ Slip-stitch folded edges.

body meets the handle, Pippa slip-stitched the folded-under edges together so the two components would appear combined. ⑦

7 Reverse appliqué the small interior circles of the large circles, and then appliqué the outer edges of the large circles. ⑧

FINISHING

1 Layer the mug rug top, batting, and backing fabric; baste the layers together. Quilt as desired.

2 Join the dark-brown solid strips end to end to make one long strip. Refer to "Binding" on page 105 to bind the mug rug edges using the joined strip.

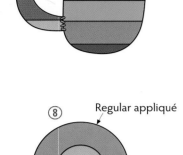

⑧ Regular appliqué

Reverse appliqué

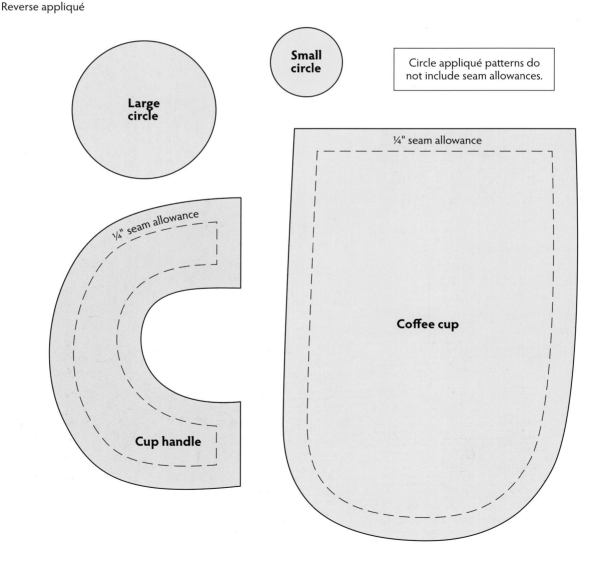

Large circle

Small circle

Circle appliqué patterns do not include seam allowances.

¼" seam allowance

Coffee cup

¼" seam allowance

Cup handle

Pointed in One Direction PILLOW

FINISHED PILLOW: 18" x 18"

Designed and made by Sarah Minshall

> If you love making quilted projects with triangles but find it hard to piece projects accurately, this pillow is for you! Instead of sewing triangles together, you sew squares on the diagonal and cut them to make half-square-triangle units. The end result is a neat take on a traditional style.
>
> ~Sarah

MATERIALS

Yardage is based on 42"-wide fabric.

⅝ yard of white solid for half-square-triangle units, border, and pillow front backing

32 squares, 3" x 3", of assorted prints for half-square-triangle units

⅝ yard of fabric for pillow back

¼ yard of fabric for binding

20" x 20" piece of cotton batting

17" of ¾"-wide Velcro

18" x 18" pillow form

CUTTING

From the white solid, cut:

32 squares, 3" x 3"

2 strips, 1" x 17½"

2 strips, 1" x 18½"

1 square, 20" x 20"

From the pillow back fabric, cut:

2 rectangles, 13" x 20"

From the binding fabric, cut:

2 strips, 2½" x 42"

ASSEMBLING THE PILLOW TOP

Use a ¼"-wide seam allowance throughout.

1 Use a pencil and ruler to draw a diagonal line from corner to corner on the wrong side of each white solid 3" square.

2 Layer each marked square with an assorted print 3" square, right sides together. Sew ¼" from both sides of the marked lines. Cut the pairs apart on the marked line. Each pair will yield two half-square-triangle units. Press the seam allowances of each pair in opposite directions. Square up each unit to 2⅝" x 2⅝". ①

3 Sew two matching half-square-triangle units together as shown. Repeat to make a total of 32 units. Don't press the seam allowances yet. ②

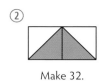
② Make 32.

4 Sew four units from step 3 together to make a row. Repeat to make a total of eight rows. ③

5 Arrange the rows so that all of the triangles are pointed in the same direction. Once you have determined the order, press the seam allowances of each row in opposite directions from row to row.

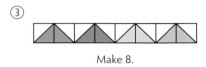
③ Make 8.

6 Sew the rows together. Press the seam allowances away from the points. ④

7 Sew the white solid 1" x 17½" strips to the sides of the pillow top. Press the seam allowances toward the strips. Sew the white solid 1" x 18½" strips to the top and bottom of the pillow top. Press the seam allowances toward the strips. ⑤

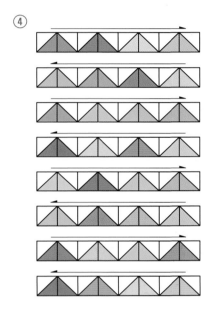
④

8 Layer the pillow top with the batting and white solid 20" backing square. Baste the layers together. Quilt as desired. Trim the quilted pillow front to 18" x 18".

MAKING THE PILLOW BACK

1 Press under ½" along one long edge of each back rectangle, and then press under 1" for the hem. Edgestitch the hem of each rectangle in place ⅛" from the fold.

2 Separate the two halves of the Velcro strip. On the right side of one backing rectangle, stitch one half of the Velcro along the hemmed edge. Sew the remaining half of the Velcro to the wrong side of the hemmed edge of the remaining back piece. Stick the Velcro together to join the back pieces.

COMPLETING THE PILLOW

1 With *wrong* sides together, stitch the quilted pillow front to the back piece, ¼" from the raw edges.

2 Sew the binding strips together end to end to make one long strip. Refer to "Binding" on page 105 to bind the pillow edges with the joined strip.

3 Insert the pillow form through the opening in the back.

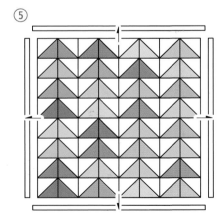
⑤

Color Punch PILLOWS

Designed and made by Heather Jones

Pink Pop White House Steps

FINISHED PILLOW: 19" x 19"

MATERIALS

Yardage is based on 42"-wide fabric.

¼ yard *each* of fuchsia, cream, gray, and light-pink solids for pillow top
½ yard of fabric for pillow backing
20" x 20" pillow form

CUTTING

From the fuchsia solid, cut:
1 square, 5½" x 5½" (A)
2 strips, 1½" x 11½" (H)
2 strips, 1½" x 13½" (I)

From the cream solid, cut:
2 strips, 1½" x 5½" (B)
2 strips, 1½" x 7½" (C)
2 strips, 1½" x 13½" (J)
2 strips, 1½" x 15½" (K)

From the gray solid, cut:
2 strips, 1½" x 7½" (D)
2 strips, 1½" x 9½" (E)
2 strips, 1½" x 15½" (L)
2 strips, 1½" x 17½" (M)

From the light-pink solid, cut:
2 strips, 1½" x 9½" (F)
2 strips, 1½" x 11½" (G)
2 strips, 1½" x 17½" (N)
2 strips, 1½" x 19½" (O)

From the backing fabric, cut:
2 rectangles, 13" x 19½"

💡 Label Your Strips

Use painter's tape to make temporary labels for all of your fabric strips in this project. Just write the letter that corresponds to the pattern on a piece of tape and adhere it to each set of strips. Then simply remove the tape as you construct each section of the pillow top.

ASSEMBLING THE PILLOW TOP

Use a ¼"-wide seam allowance throughout.

Sew the cream B strips to the top and bottom of the fuchsia A square. Press the seam allowances open. Sew the cream C strips to the sides of the A square. Press the seam allowances open. Working in alphabetical order, continue adding strips to the square, joining strips to the top and bottom first and then to the sides. Press all the seam allowances open. ①

COMPLETING THE PILLOW

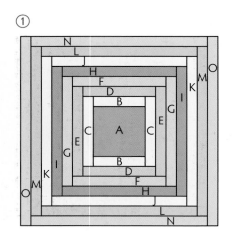

1 Press under ½" along one short side of each backing rectangle, and then press under 1½" for the hem. Edgestitch the hem of each rectangle in place ⅛" from the fold.

2 Place the pillow top on your work surface, right side up. Lay the back pieces over the top with the raw edges aligned and the hemmed edges overlapping in the middle. Adjust the overlap until the back pieces are the same size as the top. Pin the pieces together.

3 Stitch ¼" from the raw edges, backstitching at the beginning and end of your seam line.

4 Turn the pillow cover right side out and insert the pillow form into the cover through the opening in the back.

Orange-and-Gray Courthouse Steps Pillow

FINISHED PILLOW: 18" x 19"

MATERIALS

Yardage is based on 42"-wide fabric.

¼ yard *each* of orange and cream solids for pillow top
⅛ yard of gray solid for pillow top
½ yard of fabric for pillow backing
18" x 18" pillow form

CUTTING

From the orange solid, cut:
1 rectangle, 3½" x 6½" (A)
2 strips, 2½" x 7½" (C)
2 strips, 2½" x 11½" (E)
2 strips, 1½" x 17½" (I)

From the cream solid, cut:
2 strips, 2½" x 6½" (B)
2 strips, 2½" x 10½" (D)
2 strips, 2½" x 14½" (F)
2 strips, 1½" x 18½" (J)

From the gray solid, cut:
2 strips, 1½" x 15½" (G)
2 strips, 1½" x 16½" (H)

From the backing fabric, cut:
2 pieces, 13" x 18½"

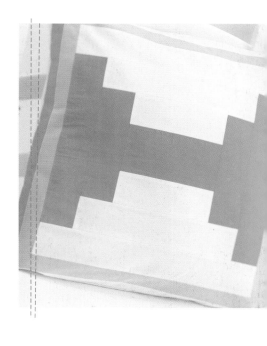

ASSEMBLING THE PILLOW TOP

Use a ¼"-wide seam allowance throughout.

Sew the cream B strips to the sides of the orange A rectangle. Press the seam allowances open. Sew the orange C strips to the top and bottom of the unit. Press the seam allowances open. Working in alphabetical order, continue adding strips to the rectangle, joining strips to the sides first, and then to the top and bottom. Press all the seam allowances open. ②

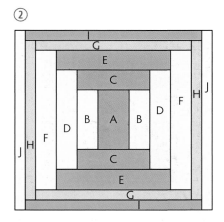

COMPLETING THE PILLOW

1 Press under ½" along one short side of each backing rectangle, and then press under 1½" for the hem. Edgestitch the hem of each rectangle in place ⅛" from the fold.

2 Place the pillow top on your work surface, right side up. Lay the backing pieces over the top with the raw edges aligned and the hemmed edges overlapping in the middle. Adjust the overlap until the backing pieces are the same size as the top. Pin the pieces together.

3 Stitch ¼" from the raw edges, backstitching at the beginning and end of your seam line.

4 Turn the pillow cover right side out and insert the pillow form into the cover through the opening in the back.

Bird on a Branch
PILLOW

FINISHED PILLOW: 16" x 12"

Designed and made by Amy Struckmeyer

MATERIALS

Yardage is based on 42"-wide fabric.

½ yard of sand-colored linen/cotton-blend fabric for pillow top and back

½ yard or 1 fat quarter (18" x 21") of brown wood-grain print for tree branch appliqué

6" x 8" rectangle *each* of felted wool sweater in 2 shades of blue for bird appliqué*

6" x 6" square of light-green felted wool sweater for leaf appliqués*

⅓ yard of 17"-wide paper-backed fusible web

Brown 6-strand embroidery floss for bird legs and eye

Size 5 embroidery needle

12" x 16" pillow form

Fabric marking pen or pencil

You can use any type of felted wool for the appliqué pieces or refer to "Felting Wool" on page 107 to felt your own yardage or wool garments.

CUTTING

From the linen/cotton-blend fabric, cut:

1 rectangle, 13" x 17"

2 rectangles, 12" x 13"

APPLIQUÉING THE PILLOW TOP

1 Using the patterns on page 101, trace one *each* of the tree branch, bird body, and bird wing shapes, and five leaf shapes onto the paper side of the fusible web. Roughly cut around each shape and fuse the pieces to the wrong side of the appropriate fabrics, following the manufacturer's instructions. Cut out each shape on the drawn line.

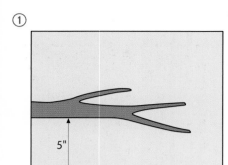

①

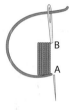

5"

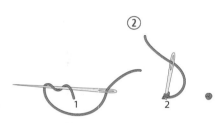

French knot

Satin stitch

2 Remove the paper backing from the tree branch shape. Fuse the shape to the 13" x 17" rectangle, aligning the raw edges on the left and placing the middle of the branch about 5" from the bottom edge. ①

3 Using matching thread, machine stitch the branch appliqué to the pillow front. Amy used a straight stitch, sewing about 1/16" from the fabric edge. This results in a slightly frayed edge, which Amy likes. If you prefer a cleaner, more finished edge, either a satin stitch or a blanket stitch is a good option.

💡 Securing the Appliqué Stitches

Rather than backstitching when sewing around the appliqués, Amy prefers to pull the thread through to the wrong side of the fabric and tie a knot. That way she can be absolutely sure the stitches are secure.

----

4 Remove the paper backing from the bird body and leaf shapes and fuse the shapes to the pillow front, referring to the photo on page 98 as needed. Using matching thread, machine stitch the appliqués in place.

5 Remove the paper backing from the wing shape and fuse it to the bird body. Machine stitch the wing in place.

6 Using three strands of embroidery floss and a satin stitch, stitch the bird's legs. Using either a satin stitch or a French knot, stitch the bird's eye. ②

COMPLETING THE PILLOW

1 Press under ½" twice along the 13"-long edge of one backing rectangle. Edgestitch the hem in place ⅛" from the fold, and then topstitch ⅜" from the fold. Repeat with the remaining backing rectangle.

2 Place the pillow top on your work surface, right side up. Lay the backing pieces over the top, right side down, with the raw edges aligned and the hemmed edges overlapping in the middle. Adjust the overlap until the backing pieces are the same size as the top. Pin the pieces together.

3 Stitch ½" from the raw edges, backstitching at the beginning and end of your seam line. Trim the corners to reduce bulk.

4 Turn the pillow cover right side out and insert the pillow form into the cover through the opening in the back.

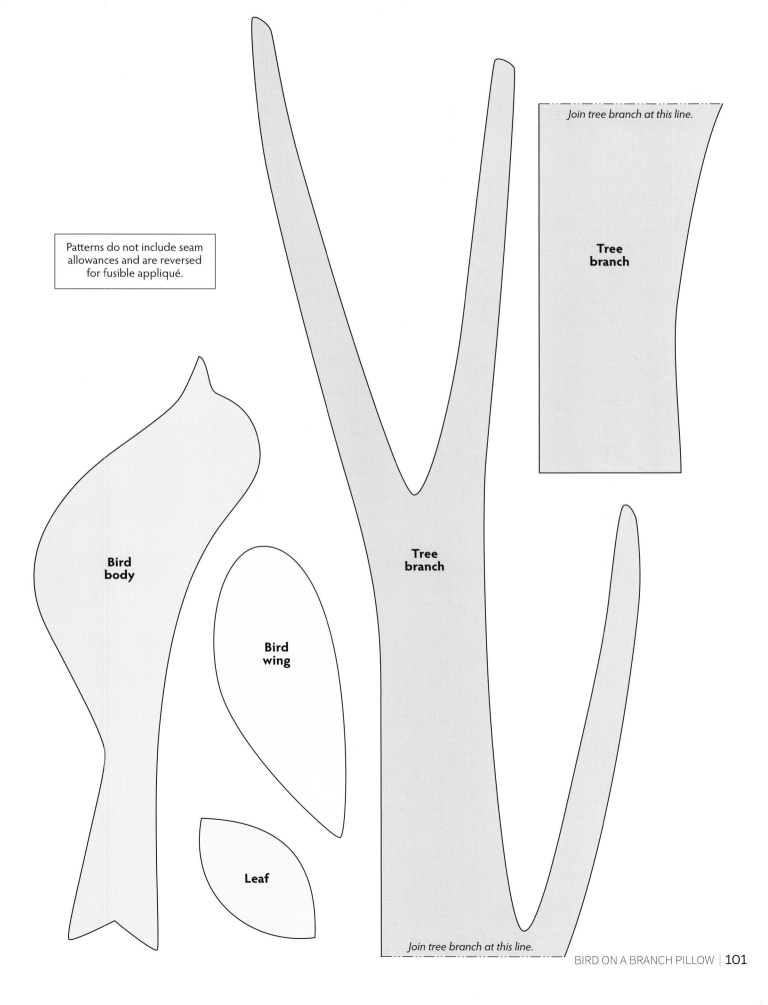

Patterns do not include seam allowances and are reversed for fusible appliqué.

Bird body

Bird wing

Leaf

Tree branch

Join tree branch at this line.

Tree branch

Join tree branch at this line.

> There's no faster or easier way to define a room than by using pillows. This bohemian chic pillow features a simple version of trendy appliqué silhouettes.
>
> ~Lauren

Vine PILLOW

FINISHED PILLOW: 18" x 18"

Designed by Lauren Jung; appliquéd and sewn by Jessi Jung

MATERIALS

Yardage is based on 42"-wide fabric.

½ yard of teal print for pillow top and back
¼ yard of brown print for stem appliqué and binding
2" x 4" rectangle *each* of 16 assorted prints for leaf appliqués
½ yard of 17"-wide paper-backed fusible web
½ yard of 12"-wide tear-away stabilizer
18" x 18" pillow form
Fabric marking pen or pencil

CUTTING

From the teal print, cut:
1 square, 18" x 18"
2 rectangles, 12" x 18"

From the brown print, cut:
2 strips, 2" x 42"

APPLIQUÉING THE PILLOW TOP

1 On the paper side of the fusible web, draw a ⅝" x 18" stem strip. Using the pattern on page 104, trace 16 leaves onto the fusible web. Roughly cut around each shape and fuse the pieces to the wrong side of the appropriate fabrics, following the manufacturer's instructions. Cut out each shape on the drawn line and remove the paper backing.

2 Fold the teal 18" square in half vertically and horizontally and crease the folds. Center the stem over the vertical crease line and fuse it in place. Equally space eight leaves on each side of the stem, leaving ½" at the top and bottom for seam allowances; fuse the shapes in place.

3 Pin or baste the stabilizer to the wrong side of the pillow top under the appliqué area. Machine blanket stitch the edges of each appliqué piece with matching or contrasting thread. ①

COMPLETING THE PILLOW

1 Press under ¼" twice along one long edge of each teal rectangle. Edgestitch the hem of each rectangle in place ⅛" from the fold.

2 Place the pillow top on your work surface, wrong side up. Lay the backing pieces over the top, right side up, with the raw edges aligned and the hemmed edges overlapping in the middle. Adjust the overlap until the backing pieces are the same size as the top. Pin the pieces together. Stitch ¼" from the raw edges.

3 Sew the brown binding strips together end to end to make one long strip. Refer to "Binding" on page 105 to bind the pillow edges with the joined strip.

4 Insert the pillow form through the opening in the back.

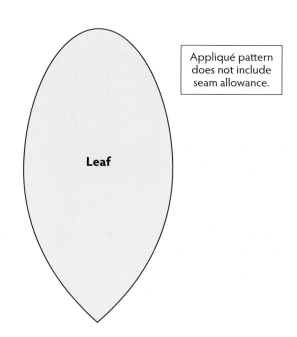

Appliqué pattern does not include seam allowance.

Leaf

Basic Sewing Techniques

Most of the projects in this book are relatively easy to make. But if any of the sewing language is unfamiliar, the information provided here may clear things up for you.

BINDING

Narrow fabric strips folded over raw edges of projects—such as wallet edges, hot pads, and more—are called binding. Binding is used to encase and finish edges, especially where there are multiple layers of fabrics and batting, as on a quilt. Binding strips are cut anywhere from 2" to 2½" wide, depending on the individual designer's preference and how thick the batting is. You may need to join strips end to end to get the length needed.

Fold the binding strip in half lengthwise, wrong sides together. Stitch the binding to the edge of the project from the right side of the project. Stop stitching ¼" from the first corner and fold the binding up at a 90° angle, and then fold it back down along the next edge of the project and continue sewing. **①**

When you near the starting point, overlap the beginning and ending tails of the binding. Mark an overlap equal to the width of your binding strip. (If your strip is 2½" wide, then mark the overlap to be 2½".) Trim the binding ends to the marked points, and then sew the ends together with a diagonal seam. **②**

Trim the excess fabric from the joined strip, leaving a ¼"-wide seam allowance. Then press the seam allowances open and stitch this last bit of binding to your project. **③**

Fold the binding over the raw edges of your project and hand stitch in place on the back side.

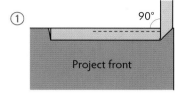

① 90°

Project front

② Overlapped ends

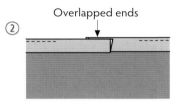

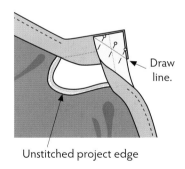

Draw line.

Unstitched project edge

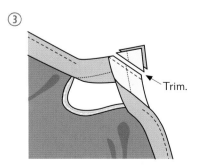

③ Trim.

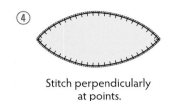

Stitch perpendicularly
at points.

BLANKET STITCH

The blanket stitch is used to secure the edges of an appliqué in a decorative manner. It can be done by hand or machine.

For machine blanket stitch, see your owner's manual to choose the correct stitch. For the stitching to show nicely, you may want to use a heavier-weight thread, such as machine quilting thread, in the machine needle. When pivoting at a corner or around a curve, pivot when the needle is in the background fabric, not in the appliqué motif, and stitch perpendicularly at points. ④

For hand blanket stitch, start with a knotted thread of pearl cotton or one or two strands of embroidery floss. Hide the knot under an appliqué piece. Bring the needle up in the background fabric at the edge of an appliqué piece. Working from left to right, insert the needle down into the appliqué and bring it back up along the edge of the appliqué, catching the thread at a right angle to the edge as shown. The thread should be underneath the needle point. Tug the thread to secure the stitch, but not so tightly that the fabric ripples. Continue stitching along the edge of the appliqué, keeping the stitch length consistent with the distance between stitches. ⑤

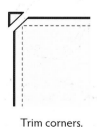

CLIPPING CURVES AND POINTS

When sewing together parts of a project that involve curves, it's much easier to make a nice, smooth seam if you clip into the seam allowances along the curved edges. For inner points, make a snip into the seam allowances before turning the pieces right side out. Trim corners, such as on a rectangular or square pillow, before turning, for nice, flat corners. When you press the pieces with the right sides out, the seam allowances will be able to lie flat. ⑥

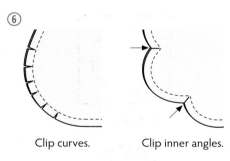

Clip curves.   Clip inner angles.

Trim corners.

EDGE STITCHING AND TOPSTITCHING

Some projects in this book use edge stitching or topstitching or both to help secure finished edges, making them lie flat and look neat. Topstitching is decorative whereas edge stitching is more functional for securing narrow edges that have been turned under or helping to keep seam allowances in place.

Edge stitching is done close to the edge of a fabric piece, as the name implies. Try to sew ⅛" or less from the edge. This is often called for when a narrow ⅛" to ¼" edge has been turned under. Topstitching is generally done ¼" from the edge of the fabric or ¼" from a row of edge stitching. ⑦

Combined edgestitching
and topstitching

FELTING WOOL

Wool needs to be felted before use to prevent it from fraying. Hand-dyed wool has already been washed, but if wool comes straight off the bolt, you'll need to wash it. The fabric must be close to 100% wool for the felting process to work. If it contains other fibers, it won't felt evenly. Wool will shrink 20% to 30% when felted, so if your wool hasn't already been felted, start with at least 30% more than you need, to allow for shrinking.

Felting is easiest to do in a top-loading washing machine—it's a combination of the water temperature and agitation that felts the wool. Use a touch of detergent to loosen the fibers. Wash the wool in hot water with a cold-water rinse and a lot of agitation. If the wool is felted enough, allow to air dry. If you want it thicker, dry in a hot dryer, checking it periodically so that you don't felt it too much. If it is not felted enough, repeat the washing process again.

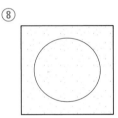

Trace pattern.

Cut loosely around shape
and cut out center.

FUSIBLE APPLIQUÉ

Fusible web provides a quick-and-easy way to adhere one fabric layer on top of another. Trace the shape you want to appliqué onto the paper side of the fusible web. Roughly cut out the shape. Following the manufacturer's instructions, iron the adhesive side of the web to the wrong side of the appliqué fabric, cut out the shape on the drawn lines, and then iron it onto the background fabric. To minimize stiffness from the adhesive, you can cut away the center of the fusible-web shape before fusing it to the appliqué fabric. ⑧

Decorative machine stitching (such as a blanket stitch or satin stitch) can be worked around the appliqué edges to make this type of appliqué quite durable—a good feature for pillows and quilts that will be laundered. As an alternative, the edges can be left unstitched on projects that won't be exposed to a lot of wear and tear, such as a wall hanging.

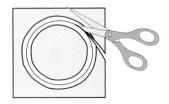

Fuse to wrong side of appliqué fabric
and cut on the drawn line.

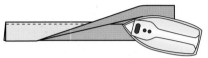

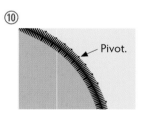

⑨

Press, lift, move, and lower
the iron along the seam.

Flip top fabric over and press.

⑩

Pivot.

Pivot when needle is outside
of the appliqué shape.

Use a narrower zigzag at points.

PRESSING

When pressing seam allowances, lift the iron before moving it, rather than gliding it back and forth over the fabric. This makes the fabric less likely to become distorted and it keeps your seam allowances from getting caught up in the edge of the iron. **⑨**

When pressing pieces involving fusible web, use a pressing cloth on top of the project to prevent the iron from becoming gummy. A nonstick appliqué pressing sheet can be used to layer and compose appliqués before fusing them to the background.

When pressing delicate fabrics such as wool or silk, use a press cloth over them to prevent scorching.

SATIN STITCHING

Machine satin stitching is one way to secure the edges of fusible appliqué. Use it when your project will get a lot of use or be washed often. Set your machine to a zigzag stitch (make sure you have an appropriate presser foot in place) and set the stitch width and length to slightly shorter and narrower than the standard setting. Sew around the appliqué shape with one swing of the needle stitching into the appliqué shape and the other swing stitching into the background fabric. **⑩**

SEAM ALLOWANCES

In this book, we've used ¼" seam allowances for patchwork, but sometimes we've used ½" seam allowances on projects that may be subjected to more stress, such as tote bags. If not specified, use a ¼" seam allowance.

ZIPPERS

Zippers are perfect for closing long openings on purses and totes as well as on pillows. And, they're relatively easy to install.

For a centered zipper that won't show, machine baste the opening closed where the zipper will be inserted and press the seam allowance open. (You'll need a ½" or ⅝" seam allowance to accommodate the width of the zipper tape.) Working from the inside or wrong side of the project, position the zipper tape face down, centering the zipper teeth over the seam line. Pin or baste each side of the zipper tape to the seam allowance only. Then from the right side of the project, topstitch in place, sewing through the project fabric and the zipper tape to secure. Remove the basting stitches along the seam line and you can now open and close the zipper. ⑪

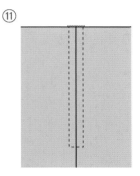

Topstitch zipper in place.

Meet the Contributors

Cinzia Allocca

Cinzia is a wife, mother, quiltmaker, and sewing instructor. She lives in Montreal, Canada, with her husband and two children. She is cofounder and president of the Montreal Modern Quilt Guild. Her work has been published in *Stitch* and *Modern Quilts Unlimited*. She sews because it fulfills her need for self-expression and for creating something that is tangible, functional, and tactile.

Cinzia blogs about her process at DeuxPetitesSouris.blogspot.com and sells her original, modern quilts at DeuxPetitesSouris.etsy.com.

Pippa Eccles Armbrester

Pippa is a quiltmaker and designer with a fondness for bold geometric designs and bright, colorful solid fabrics. Her work focuses on patterns that balance the tradition of quilting and patchwork with a fun, whimsical, and contemporary approach. She believes in a fuss-free and joyful attitude regarding the quilt-making process, one that emphasizes heartfelt quilts meant to be used rather than perfect technique. She lives and works in Boston with her husband, Kyle, and her tiny teacup poodle, Martin. Pippa enjoys cooking and baking (bread especially), attends frequent hot yoga classes, and loves long (but slow) runs by the Charles River. Knitting and crochet are her portable needlework of choice. She blogs at PippaPatchwork .com and sells her quilts online at etsy.com/shop /PippaPatchwork.

Josée Carrier

Josée has worked in the engineering field and is currently a stay-at-home mom. In her free time, you can find her in her sewing room. She loves creating with fabrics and threads and designing projects of her own. She has found a great way to express her creativity through quilting and patchwork projects. She is part of the Modern Quilt Guild and cofounder of its Montreal branch. If you want to learn more about her projects, visit her at TheCharmingNeedle.com.

Lesley Chaisson

Lesley has been sewing since she was eight, when she began making little doll clothes. She made her first quilt when she was 14 and still has some of the fabrics she began collecting as a child. Lesley is the author of *Charmed I'm Sure* (Martingale, 2009), and has published many patterns in various crafting and quilting magazines.

Elizabeth Dackson

Elizabeth is a self-proclaimed fabric addict and modern quilter. She designs quilt patterns, which you can find on her blog, Don't Call Me Betsy (DontCallMeBetsy.com), as well as in various quilting publications, including *Quiltmaker*, *International Quilt Festival: Quilt Scene*, and *Fat Quarterly*. She is also an active member of the Tampa Modern Quilt Guild and is the author of *Becoming a Confident Quilter* (Martingale, 2013). Elizabeth lives in Florida with her husband, son, and neurotic beagle.

Linda Turner Griepentrog

Linda loves all things fabric and fiber—just look in her sewing room and closets! Since graduating from Oregon State University, she's had a varied career in the sewing industry. As a designer, writer, and editor, she works with several companies in the sewing, crafting, and quilting communities. Linda is the author of five books and thousands of magazine articles. She loves to solve sewing challenges and believes that, given enough time and thought, she can construct anything! Linda, her husband (conveniently, a fabric-store manager), and three dogs live in Bend, Oregon.

Debbie Grifka

Debbie has been sewing all her life and quilting for the past 10 years. Her designs have appeared in such magazines as *Stitch*, *Quilting Arts Gifts*, and

Modern Patchwork, and she publishes her own patterns under the name Esch House Quilts. Debbie's quilt "Ephemeral Elegance," which uses her bias-appliqué technique, won first place in its category in the American Quilter's Society Quilt Show in Paducah in 2011. She is an active member of the social-media community and you can visit her blog at EschHouseQuilts.blogspot.com.

Heather Jones

Heather is a designer and modern quilter. She lives in Cincinnati with her husband, Jeff, and two young children, Aidan and Olivia, who are her biggest supporters, as well as her greatest sources of inspiration. Heather founded the Cincinnati chapter of the Modern Quilt Guild and she recently completed her first line of quilting patterns. Three of her original quilts were chosen as winners of the Modern Quilt Guild's Project Modern challenges, a yearlong national quilting competition. For more information on Heather and her work, please visit her blog at OliveandOllie.com.

Lauren Jung and Jessi Jung

Lauren and Jessi are fabric designers for Moda Fabrics, as well as pattern developers. Lauren is a graphic artist and Jessi is a quiltmaker. What better way for this mother-daughter team to share a love for sewing and fabric than to combine their skills in a working relationship? Their graphics center around nature with an organic feel, and their fabric colors tend to be bright and punchy. Their project patterns appeal to all ages, tastes, and skill levels. Check them out at LaurenandJessiJung.com.

Sarah Minshall

Sarah is a quilter, sewer, and maker of all things fabric related. She began quilting in college as a way to relieve stress and as a way to make a unique gift for her boyfriend (now husband) on a student's budget. Sarah is inspired by great color and modern design and thinks quilting and patchwork should be incorporated into more than just quilts. Sarah lives in Michigan with her husband, dog, and cat. Keep tabs on what she's making at her website: HipToPieceSquares.com.

April Moffatt

April is married to an amazing man, is a mom of four children ages 9 to 16 whom she homeschools, and is a writer and teacher of all things sewing related. Her patterns regularly appear in national publications, allowing April to share her designs with other people who love to sew. She sells her patterns and shares many sewing tips on her website at AprilMoffattDesign.com.

Gail Pan

Gail lives in the Dandenong Ranges on the outskirts of Melbourne, Australia, with her husband and three boys. She's been sewing all her life and started designing when her kids were small. Gail has had various jobs but decided a few years ago to make designing a full-time job. She has met amazing people along the way and has been able to visit the most gorgeous places as part of her business. Gail teaches all around Australia and also overseas. She loves to inspire people to enjoy the world of patchwork, stitching, and quilting. You can follow Gail at GailPanDesigns.typepad.com.

Missy Shepler

Missy is the coauthor of *The Complete Idiot's Guide to Sewing*. Whenever possible, Missy combines her "day job" as a designer, author, and illustrator with her love of stitching by creating projects, patterns, and illustrations for sewing and quilting clients and publications. See what she's stitching up now at MissyStitches.com.

Adrienne Smitke

Adrienne grew up in a house full of handmade quilts and clothes. Her mother taught her to sew at an early age, even assigning her sewing "homework" over one summer vacation—she made a rad pair of black-and-neon green shorts (it was the '80s, after all). Drawing on her creative childhood, Adrienne studied illustration and graphic design in college, during which she finally began experimenting with sewing again on her own. She coauthored her first book, *Everyday Handmade* (Martingale, 2011), with her friend Cassie Barden. Visit their website at HandmadeIsAwesome.com. You can see more of Adrienne's patterns in *A Baker's Dozen* (2010), *Jelly Babies* (2011), *Sew the Perfect Gift* (2011), and *Quilting with Fat Quarters* (2012), all from Martingale.

Amy Struckmeyer

Amy lives just outside of Chicago with her husband and two strong-willed and creative children. Her love for textiles and creating began early in her Waldorf School education with lessons in knitting, weaving, and sewing. An architect by profession, she now uses her design and drawing skills to create modern sewing projects and patterns, some of which have appeared in *Stitch* magazine. She recently fell in love with screen printing and wishes she had the space to properly print yards of fabric. One of these days, she just might sew her first quilt. Visit her at FormWorkDesign.blogspot.com.